Awakening to Wildfire:
Stories of the Mendocino Lake Complex Fire

Edited by Jannah Minnix

Ukiah Valley Friends of the Library
Ukiah, California

Awakening to Wildfire:
Stories of the Mendocino Lake Complex Fire
© 2019 Ukiah Valley Friends of the Library

Ukiah Valley Friends of the Library
105 N. Main Street, Ukiah, CA 95482
http://ukiahfol.com
Cover design by Cypress House / Charles Hathaway
Cover photo by CAL FIRE
Interior map by Rixanne Wehren
Book Production by Cypress House
www.cypresshouse.com

Library of Congress Control Number: 2019911898

ISBN: 978-0-578-53266-0

Printed in the USA

First Printing 2019

2 4 6 8 9 7 5 3 1

First Edition

For
Steve — Janet — Jane
Charle — Margaret — Roy
Irma — Kai — Kressa

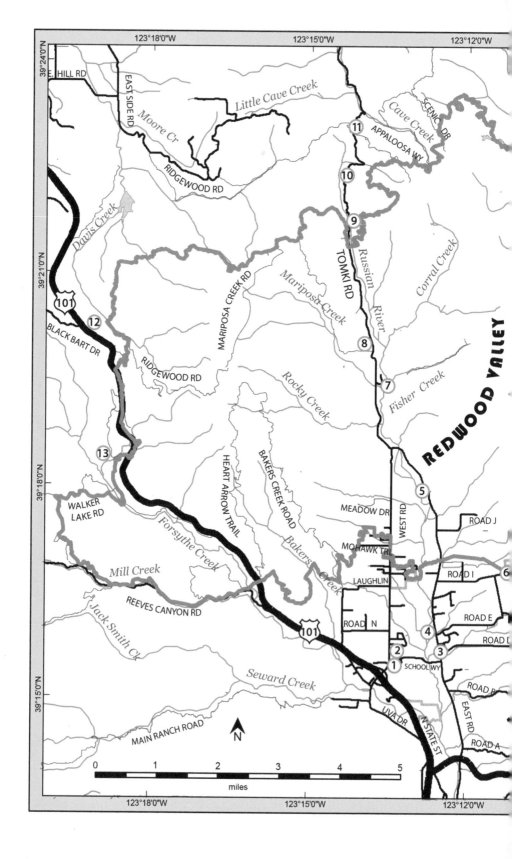

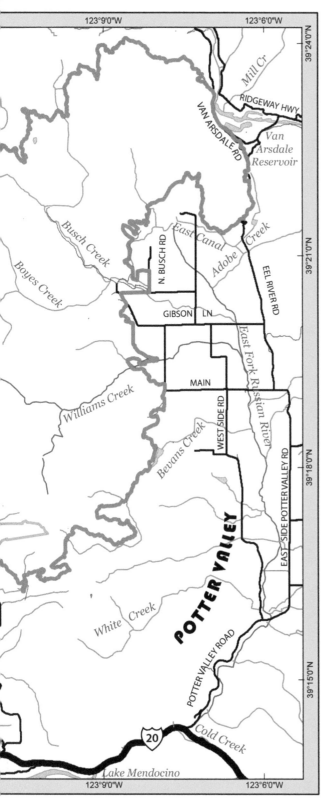

Redwood Valley Fire Of 2017

(Mendocino Complex)

Legend

- 2017 fire perimeter
- streams
- highways
- public paved roads
- private dirt roads
- Native American lands
- (#) selected sites

1 Koh HaEmek Jewish Comm.
2 Eagle Peak Middle School
3 Post Office, Market, Fire Dept.
4 Lions Club Park
5 RV Gravel & Wastewater
6 RV Rancheria offices
7 Fisher Lake Dr. residences
8 Frey Vineyards
9 Abhayagiri Buddhist
   Monastery
10 Mt. Tabor Monastery
11 Tomki summit
12 Ridgewood summit
13 Golden Rule RV park

Rixanne Wehren
Cartographer 2019

Sources: Calfire, Mendocino
County, CalGIS, ESRI ArcMap

Table of Contents

Table of Contents

Acknowledgments

This book was made possible through a grant from the Redwood Valley and Santa Rosa Community Recovery Fund. Deepest thanks go to the Recovery Fund committee for selecting this project, and the Community Foundation of Mendocino County for administering the funds for us to see the book through to completion.

Michele Savoy and the Ukiah Valley Friends of the Library are owed much gratitude: for their expertise in the book industry, being the official name on the grant, their continual support and enthusiasm for the project, and helping to keep the project rolling.

Without the writing wizardry of Carole Brodsky and the photographical and writing prowess of Ree Slocum, this book would be an awful lot smaller. Thank you, Ree and Carole, for the time you spent talking with our community and recording their stories, for your incredible attitudes, your initiative, your listening ears, and for being part of this team. I couldn't have pulled this together without you.

Thank you to our poets laureate past and present, Michael Riedell, Theresa Whitehill, and Linda Noel for volunteering your time and mentorship in leading multiple poetry workshops. Your guidance, prompts, and ability to create a safe sharing space helped inspire others to manifest their stories through poetry.

Thank you to Cynthia Frank from Cypress House for guiding me along the publishing process and answering my newbie's myriad of questions. You have been a fount of patience, a wonder and a blessing to work with.

There are so many others who helped inspire and encourage this project, from sharing stories to helping peer-review the grant in its draft stages, emotional support and more. The Out of the Ashes/Art from the Ashes group, Ann and Gerald Croissant, Heidi and Brian Croissant, Joey Minnix, Tiffany Newton, Rose Bell, Melissa Eleftherion Carr and the staff of the Mendocino County Library, Ukiah Branch and Administrative Staff, Ellen Weed, Danilla Sands and members of the Potter Valley/Redwood Valley Fire 2017 – Mendocino Fire Alerts/Resources Facebook group, Jo-ann Rosen, Anne Shirako, Maureen Gatt, California H.O.P.E., Tricia Austin, Chris Pugh, the Ukiah Daily Journal, CAL FIRE, Mendocino County Sheriff's Office and other first responders, and anyone who helped spread the word about this project, listened to me babble about it, or told your story through words or pictures and became part of it. All of you were critical pieces that put Awakening to Wildfire together.

My most heartfelt thanks to all of you.

Introduction

I was on my way home from the voyage of a lifetime, an all-expenses-reimbursed work trip to a massive book fair in Madrid to buy books in Spanish for the library. Aside from proximity to some Catalonian protests, the unsettling sight of police with assault rifles everywhere, fear of pickpockets, being less than fluent in the primary spoken language, and the paranoia that all of this was too good to be true and something awful or seedy was bound to come up (my coworkers and I even had a "farewell" gathering before the trip because part of me was terrified I'd somehow die or disappear forever), everything had been like a dream. One of the librarians I'd met at the book fair would be going back to the States to deal with flood damage from Hurricane Harvey, but otherwise we looked forward to going home to share the good news of our finds, the swag we'd accumulated, and the treats we'd bought for our coworkers, friends, and families. There had been no actual problems. No one accosted me or stole my stuff, my luggage wasn't lost, the Airbnb hosts were wonderful, the book fair was great, no food poisoning, no one was even rude—really, it had all been fine.

The plane touched down at London Gatwick for what I anticipated to be a dull four-hour layover. I turned on my phone and trudged slowly through customs, then headed up to the food court for breakfast.

Before 10 a.m. London time (2 a.m. in Redwood Valley), I got a weird text: UPDATE ON REDWOOD VALLEY AND POTTER VALLEY FIRES—MANDATORY EVACUATIONS. Another fire in Redwood Valley? The text went on to list the names of evacuated streets and directions I didn't really understand, still being new to Redwood Valley's layout. The airport offered thirty minutes' free Wi-Fi and I took it, hopping onto Facebook to see my coworker and neighbor, Jen, ask if anyone else had gotten the alert.

"Please tell me that evac order doesn't include us," I texted her.

"It includes us," she responded two minutes later.

"Shit!"

I forwarded the message to my husband, Joey, back home.

A minute passed. Two. Too many for comfort.

I called Joey. He answered, and it was obvious my call had woken him. He read my texts while I had him on the phone, and I told him we were part of the evacuation area and he had to get out of the house. We'd packed go-bags and taken photos of our belongings for insurance earlier in the summer during a previous fire scare, and between the two of us he was the ever-rational, level-headed one, so I knew he was as prepared as he was going to be, but not being there by his side, to go through this together, devastated me. I was forced to sit there, tell him I loved him, hang up, and wait for the text that he'd made it somewhere safe.

Then Jen called to check on me.

"Where are you?" she asked.

"London!" I replied, half-laughing, half-crying.

I told her I'd called Joey and he was evacuating, got the update on her family and their goats, then disconnected.

Joey finally texted that he'd made it to his friend's house in Ukiah, and I released a shaky breath of relief.

I struggled to stay connected, obsessively refreshing Facebook for updates and found that someone had posted a link to the emergency services scanners. I wandered the airport with the scanner whispering fragments of Armageddon in my ears while everyone else around me went about their business, completely oblivious that a little community on the other side of the world was going up in flames.

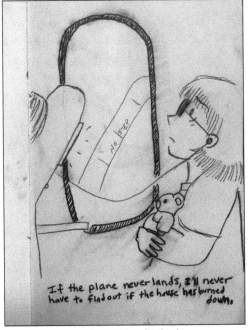

If the plane never lands, I'll never have to find out if the house has burned down.

Drawing from the flight home.

And then my Wi-Fi time was up, and my connection to home was severed.

The next eleven hours were agonizing, the worst season-finale cliffhanger. Schrödinger's town—it was both totally fine and totally destroyed at the same time, so long as you stayed in limbo up in the sky. I'd bought sleeping pills at the airport pharmacy to try to knock myself out on the flight, but being on the verge of an anxiety attack the entire time, they did virtually nothing.

I tried to distract myself, but my thoughts were drawn to home like ultra-polarized magnets. There was a stuffed bear that I'd purchased with the intent of giving as a gift, but he ended up cradled in my arms and soaked in fretful tears. I named him Arthur, both because I got him at the London airport and because I hoped he'd help bolster my courage (he didn't). I doodled listlessly and watched the display on the back of the seat in front of me count down the hours to home. I saw smoke at one point when we finally started flying over California. Was that us? I wondered.

At Oakland International Airport, going through customs again, people had begun to hear about the fires, but they were almost all talking about Sonoma County. Murmurs of loved ones living in affected areas, freeway closures, and what had burned vs. what had survived, echoed through the serpentine line. Then I was out at baggage claim at last, ready to board the shuttle to take me to my car at Charles M. Schulz-Sonoma County Airport in Santa Rosa—except there was no shuttle, and no one answered their phone line. It sounded like Highway 101 was shut down. Joey said it might be a good idea to spend the night in Oakland and try again the next day, so that's what I ended up doing. I barricaded my hotel-room door out of sheer anxiety.

On Tuesday the shuttle was running again. The group of us passengers stood solemnly at the waiting area, sharing tissues as we tried to steel ourselves for the journey to Sonoma County and what lay in store for us there. The bus arrived, and the driver confirmed over their radio system that Sonoma County Airport was open, so I'd be able to get my car

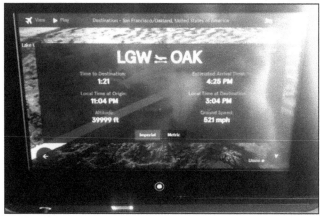

Flight display on the plane. Photo by Jannah Minnix.

out. The way to Ukiah reconstructed itself in segments.

Smoke infiltrated the bus and got progressively worse the farther north we got. I breathed into my scarf, clutching Arthur tightly. Even with Dramamine in my system and motion-sickness pressure cuffs on, my stomach still lurched. When we reached Santa Rosa, it was like entering an alternate reality. Parts of the freeway shoulders still smoldered and smoked. One business was demolished, while the framework of an unfinished building across the street was untouched. Acres of charred earth suddenly stopped and gave way to bright green vineyards, still full of life. It was the strangest, most otherworldly thing.

Destroyed building. Photo by Jannah Minnix.

We got to the Sonoma County airport, and as we parted ways wished each other good luck in whatever happened next. People sat outside the building; as I came to discover it was because the airport had no power.

Untouched building. Photo by Jannah Minnix.

There was no way to manage the long-term parking, so the exits had been opened to allow people to go freely. "Can I use your bathroom before I leave?" I asked one of the airport employees seated on the stairs.

"Do you have a flashlight?" he asked.

I had my phone, and that was good enough, so I was allowed inside the blacked-out airport to pee in the darkness.

Then I had my car back—I could go home!

No, wait—I could go to Joey's friend's house.

But I could see Joey, and see that he was okay. That would be huge.

Then a thought crept into my head: you know who's probably exhausted, and working crazy shifts, and totally forgotten about right now? The dispatchers. Before becoming a children's librarian, I was a 9-1-1 dispatcher. When terrible things happen and work gets super-intense and demanding, the emergency dispatchers pick up the slack. They notoriously work insane hours, sometimes with no breaks, and some had likely been evacuated. By this point they'd been answering hundreds of calls from people experiencing the worst days of their lives, and vicariously living everyone else's trauma, and while everyone thanked the firefighters, few remembered to thank the dispatchers. I decided to make a care-package run; Wal-Mart in Santa Rosa happened to be open, so I drove there for supplies.

You think Wal-Mart is nuts on a good day? Try going there in the midst of a crisis.

Panicked or dazed people ran or stood around everywhere, carts piled high with food and anything else they could carry. All the water was completely gone. Other food and beverage items were getting low. Various items had fallen and lay like waste on the ground.

I went for the caffeine and comfort foods: Monster, Red Bull, sodas, Gatorade, chocolate, etc.—not the healthiest stuff, but the kinds of snacks my coworkers and I had reached for ten hours into our shifts to keep us going. A woman walked up and asked me if my house was all right. "I don't know," I replied. "What about yours?"

She shook her head. "Everything's gone."

"I'm so sorry." My eyes watered. I wanted to hold her, hug her as hard as I could, but then she was gone.

I made it back to Ukiah and checked in at the library. Everyone was accounted for. Jen and another coworker and a couple volunteers had been evacuated but were safe. Some colleagues offered Joey and me a place to stay. A few coworkers had tried to open the library on Monday to collect and offer clothing to fire survivors, till management forced them to close. The Willits library was the only place in Willits with Internet access. Both libraries were in use as impromptu community meeting points where you could check your email, bump into neighbors, see them safe, and exchange stories and information. I thought it would be so neat if we could try to collect those stories somehow, but everything was so raw and the fires were still raging—it was something to think about.

Joey and I reunited and made a run up to our house. We lived on the south end of Redwood Valley, and today the roadblock had been adjusted so the cutoff was right at our turn, Road B. We pulled into our driveway where our house stood, perfectly fine in the smoky haze, and quickly grabbed some more possessions to bring to our friend's house: photo albums, clothes, my bagpipes. Then we headed back to Ukiah. With the help of friends and acquaintances I got the snack-and-caffeine care package to the dispatchers at the sheriff's office, and thanked them for all they were doing. Finally, after a week, Joey and I got to return home.

Our side of Redwood Valley made it out physically unscathed by the fire, but at the library we encountered many patrons who'd suffered. We offered N-95 masks, our ears, shoulders to cry on, a safe place to gather, our regular storytimes, therapy dogs, and book clubs—whatever we could think of to try to help, but there was still so much pain. I wanted to try to figure out what would help others heal from the trauma the fire had caused.

Some people confided that every time they told their story, they felt a little better, so I took that and ran with it. We looked into StoryCorps—too expensive. In hopes of doing some kind of storytelling archival project, we applied to the California Listens group through the California State Library. While Mendocino County wasn't specifically selected for our own venture, we did get to participate in what ended up being their "California Wildfires Story Project" and recorded fifteen video interviews with all kinds of people. These were then edited, excerpted, and added to a state archive of interviews with people who'd faced fires all over the state. I was hoping for something more personal for our community, though—an archive that preserved the history of the event from many points of view, conveyed through whatever medium the storyteller needed for the purpose of healing from the fire. Thus the Mendocino Fire Story project was born.

What you hold here is a compilation of narratives, interviews, poetry, photographs, and artwork that tells the story of the Mendocino Lake Complex Fire, also known as the Redwood Valley Fire, which began at 11:36 p.m. on October 8, 2017. It burned 36,523 acres, destroyed 546 structures, and claimed the lives of nine. Tucked in the poetry section, you'll find a couple additional voices from our neighbors in Lake County, who describe their lives in the wake of the Ranch Fire, showing that we share the same fears, pain, and contemplations.

This book isn't a walk in the park. It's not meant to be. It may hurt. It may stir up some feelings and memories in you, and that's not entirely bad. Hopefully, it's cathartic, and going through each piece gradually helps take some of the edge off the pain. Please be kind to yourself, though, and know when to pause to digest. There's a lot to process.

I hope this book reminds you that you aren't alone; you have a whole community recovering with you. We all mourn and heal at our own pace, and that's okay.

If there's one continuing theme you'll notice, it's that there are tons of people out here ready to support you with a cup of coffee, or at least a hug, and are glad you're safe.

I am so glad you're safe,
Jannah

A Halloween note Margaret Stephenson sent oddly early to her friend, Jennie Barker, just before Margaret lost her life in the October 2017 fire.

Narratives

Fire, Trauma, and Reclamation
Vivian Sotomayor Power

During Thanksgiving week of 2017 I found myself in the cool, humid air of Seattle, where I'd escaped to be with my daughters and their families. One morning we visited an exquisite waterfall in the area. A short hike took us down a trail to the bottom of a massive wall of water that pounded against the rock, thundering so loud that it drowned out our words. The misty spray felt refreshing as I tried to absorb the magnificent beauty. At the same time, I felt restless and didn't understand why. Eventually, I realized that the deafening sounds of the crashing water frightened me—they mimicked the roar of the fire that had threatened my life the month before. I was witnessing the effects of trauma and the strong imprint that the Redwood Complex fire had left on my psyche.

The fire that impacted our community so profoundly invaded my land on its eastern horizon as it crept up and over the hills that separate my little valley from the town of Potter Valley. Since then I have gotten this habit of often scanning these hilltops, the place where this story began. In the times before the fire, I favored the western horizon with its colorful fiery sunsets. I hardly ever watched sunrises and mostly sought the east on nights of full moon.

Today, on the tops of the scarred eastern hills, a few spots of green dot the monotonous straw background, and on the skyline stand out the silhouettes of three or four conifer skeletons, ceremonial totems still standing to mark a time and place. Not long ago, before spring came, the tops of the hills were in mourning, shrouded by the ominous black mantle of the scorched fields. This was the landscape that followed that fateful early Monday hour when I first saw the fire from my bedroom window. Raging tongues of flame towered over the top of the range like an erupting volcano, then cascaded down like lava flows threatening me, my house, my reality. It was an image of the destructive side of power that's etched permanently in my brain and often evokes that most frightening masterpiece, Goya's "Saturn Devouring his Son."

The eve of the fire had been a beautiful Indian summer day, a free Sunday for lingering in my garden and enjoying the sun while taking care of end-of-the-year garden chores. It was my lucky day, when at long last I made phone contact with a friend in my little town of Rincón, Puerto Rico. Just the month before, two historically huge hurricanes had devastated the island. For my friend, this was the first day after the hurricane that he was able to communicate by phone. He told me he would go to the barrio early the next day, check on my house there, and call me to report on how it had fared.

In the evening, I had a call from my dear soul friend from México. It was always comforting to hear her sweet, soothing voice checking on me. Earlier in the year I had lost my husband, the light of my life, and she called periodically to console me. That night I confided in her that, for the first time, I had started to believe in the possibility that someday I would recover my former life rhythms, lost after my tragedy. We talked till eleven p.m. and then I went to sleep.

My friend in Puerto Rico never understood why I didn't pick up the phone the next day when he called to report on my house. Little did we know that by the next morning it was my turn, here in California, to lose my phone connection for months. Meanwhile, my friend in México couldn't believe her eyes when she read my Facebook posts early the next morning. Little did we know that, less than two hours after we hung up, wildfire would strike.

After I went to bed, I heard the wind blow wildly against my house. I thought it would be best to get up and check, but exhaustion won over, and I fell into a deep sleep. The next thing I heard was the loud shouts of a male voice outside my bedroom door. I froze in horror. After I recognized his voice, a former neighbor who remembered that I was alone at the end of the road, closest to the fire source, I breathed a sigh of relief. He told me about the fire, but I was in disbelief. I reasoned that fires were common and likely controllable. He asked me to look out the window, and then I saw this giant monster, looming on top of the mountain, an image of evil whose presence made me feel insignificantly small and doomed. But if there was a menacing devil outside, there was a guardian angel inside, calming me down with kind words, guiding me, strategizing for me, and assuring me we had time to escape.

From there on all hell broke loose. I thought there were some good spirits in the mix, but their presence was obscured at the time. I started to drive out in my best car, the one with the lowest clearance, but stopped upon realizing that I'd left the house lights on. Solar living trains you not to waste energy. Maybe I just needed an excuse to delay leaving. I forced myself to let it go and took one long last look. My home was festive with the lights on in the dark of the night. I muttered a silent farewell. Perhaps it was a prayer. Then reality sunk in and I was assaulted by the thought that the fast-moving firestorm could soon close off my only exit. Fear conquered reluctance and I swiftly rode out, leaving my beautiful place behind.

For two miles of dirt road I watched the fire running parallel to my route, speeding in the same direction I was going. By the time I reached the pavement, the fire had won the race and had taken over both sides of the road. This forced me to turn north into old Tomki, which is more like a creek bed strewn with big boulders. I had been on it years before, when my husband drove us through for a family picnic on his birthday, but that night it became alien territory. There was enormous pressure from the long row of cars behind me, all fleeing the fire as I was, but my car's low clearance handicapped me. Then, suddenly I was on a deserted road and knew I'd lost my spatial orientation because all the other cars had vanished. I turned back blindly, seeking the company of my fellow travelers, and, after what seemed an eternity, rejoined them. I wanted to talk to someone and tried my phone, waking up my unsuspecting daughter in Seattle after I managed to weakly cry out her name. Then the call dropped, leaving my daughter in a state of panic. The absurdity of the situation had a surrealistic quality. I lost all track of time and was in the middle of gridlock, in the middle of darkness, in an endless maze of rough dirt roads that I couldn't navigate.

At last my wheels touched the pavement, and I snapped out of my altered state. I had finally arrived at a safe harbor. I would take the freeway and head south to where I had to be that Monday. Surely the authorities were monitoring the freeway and would block it if there was danger. Confidently, I took the open entrance and soon noticed that, except for my car and the one behind me, the road was empty. I reached the summit, and on the way down descended into an inferno engulfing both sides of the freeway. Only the guardrails held back the conflagration. Flying cinders bombarded my windshield, and a growing screen of smoke was blindfolding me. I thought this was it; things were coming quickly to the end. All I could do was keep my foot on the gas and close my eyes to the fact that I was trapped with a tank full of gasoline between two walls of flame.

I don't remember how long my torment lasted. Stunned and exhausted, I parked my car at a bus stop on the freeway exit closest to my house and planned to spend the night there. By morning, the firemen would have things under control and I could go home. Then, my daughter, who by now had been updated, called and advised me to go to a motel, an obvious option far from my mind. I got one of the last rooms available, but sleep was impossible. I decided to check myself safe on Facebook to inform my family near and far, and then my body finally caught my attention. I was shaking violently, partly because I didn't have a coat with me, and I noticed a painful lump in my throat. I let out a long cry, and the dam holding back my tears cracked open. They were tears of fear, of relief, of gratitude, of exhaustion. They were tears mainly of loneliness. I knew, because all night I had been subconsciously aware, that no one else was traveling alone. I missed my husband, his protection, his strength.

During the following nine days, many of us were in limbo. I knew nothing of my house, let alone of my future. Some asked if I would rebuild, assuming that my house had burned down. Others told me to prepare myself for the worst because everything else in my neighborhood had perished. In the choir of voices pulling me in all directions, I came up with a simple mantra that held me through: Whatever happened, it's going to be okay. I called on it when fear assaulted me or when I broke down, which was often. What became most important was that "for now" I needed to believe that things would work out; the "how" would come later and presently it was irrelevant. But what truly sustained me through this period was the outpouring of generosity and kindness from those who hugged me, who sheltered me, who fed me, who contacted me, both my physical and virtual communities. I was moved by the patience of my students and the administration, who put up with my frequent absences, giving me time off when I needed it. I was delighted when my daughter and my niece brought me clothes of all types. Here in the midst of lack I had a new wardrobe for all occasions. There were many blessings and I was thankful.

Finally, the day of reckoning came. I could return to my place and see what was or wasn't there. Seated between two loving friends, I rode up the two-mile dirt road. All around there were dead trees and expanses of scorched fields. As we got closer, I held tightly onto my friends' hands. I saw the first casualty and my heart cried for my barn that was no more. Then, as we neared the end of the road, surrounded by charred structures, twisted metal, and blackened vegetation, there stood my lovely home in all its glory, intact, without a smudge or smoke damage. Even the firemen couldn't explain why it survived. Indeed, the good spirits had been there, and without a doubt one of them was my protector, watching over our treasures.

I couldn't move back until the end of November, after I'd recovered the spring water thanks to the help of the most generous of friends and family. Later, also through the mediation of a good friend, I got propane and then my phone line, but it wasn't till February that I had the magic of lights, making my house festive again, and the Internet, to connect me with the rest of the world. The restoration of services has been slow and sometimes painful. A year later, I'm still struggling to reach square one. When will I get there?

A year has passed, and many survivors find themselves at crossings they never fathomed. The fire is a constant that impacts daily life because the traumatic effects of disaster aren't limited to the actual events themselves. One must also cope with the insidious stress of submitting paperwork to insurance companies and government agencies; one must deal with the endless details of recovery projects, negotiate with contractors, make the numerous decisions survivors must make, worry about the high cost of everything. At stake are numerous new responsibilities, large investments of time, and a drain of resources. I've learned much from the process, but I long for the end of this phase, or at least for a point of equilibrium.

I've been mostly treated with fairness, but there are exceptions. In this post-fire phase some have taken advantage of survivors' vulnerabilities; in my case, perhaps because of ethnic and racial differences, or maybe because of my accent, or simply because I'm an elderly woman who lacks a man to stand by her. I even hired a male friend to be present when someone who I felt disrespected me was due on the premises. The mix of adverse circumstances of my new life has left me exposed. My only defense is to keep on learning. Fortunately, for the few who've done wrong, there are many kindhearted souls, enlightened by the generosity of the human spirit. They fill me with hope and inspiration.

Earlier, I alluded to how a couple of hours before the fire, I shared with my friend the feeling of a possibility: I could begin to reclaim some of my former life rhythms that abandoned me after the loss of my husband. The obliteration of that feeling was one of the biggest casualties of this fire. After losing so much in 2017—from fire, from hurricanes, from the departure of my love—I presume that what upholds me derives from a strong survival instinct. It was what saved me on the freeway; what keeps me sane in the midst of chaos; an urge that energizes me and, hopefully, leads me into the mindset that uproots trauma and heals the soul. A first step would be to reclaim that feeling I spoke of the night before the events on the morning of October 9, 2017. Disasters can snatch it all, but they cannot impede the human spirit from rising out of the ashes and soaring high into the realm of new possibilities.

Photo by Debbie Schmidt.

Baseball found, untouched, among the ashes. Photo by Debbie Schmidt.

A Wakeup Call
Anonymous

Monday October 9, 2017

It's 1:30 a.m. and pitch-black. I'm in a deep sleep. The doorbell rings. Really? It rings again, so I get up to answer it. Katrena,[1] my neighbor, stands there, mute, eyes wide with fear. Oblivious of what will unfold in the next few minutes, I ask what's wrong. She whispers, "Fire" and points to the back of the house, the east. I look, and see flames coming down the hillside. Stunned, I turn to say something to Katrena, but she's gone, on a mission to wake our other neighbors on Fisher Lake Drive.

I can't think straight, and I'm terrified. The noise of the fire is relentless and without pity: unbelievably loud, an incessant whirr, whirr, whirr; smoke, flames, falling branches. I gather up some clothes, a photo of my late husband, my passport, my purse, and hastily try to dress. Suddenly I think of my expensive Mac computer; I try to unplug it, but all the wires are beyond my ken. I must have opened the garage door, but I don't remember doing that. The front door is still open. Another neighbor, Dave Kim, rushes in, shouting at me, "Get out now!" If he hadn't, I'd be dead. Then the lights go out, and I'm left in blackness with the ever-present din of the firestorm raging around my ears. I shake off my stupor, grab what I can, and get in the car. All this has taken maybe five minutes; the flames are now licking along the grass at the front of the house, and the horrific whirlwind continues to engulf me. I'm in the car, driving out on West Road, following the taillights of a car in front. The lights become obscured from time to time because of the thick, swirling smoke. Please, oh please, don't let me lose sight of those taillights. Burning branches continue to fall in the road and I am terrified I'll drive into a ditch.

I don't remember turning from West Road onto East Road, but I must have done so. The car I've been following pulls up at what I now recognize as Redwood Market Place. Other cars and trucks are there, the occupants silent and in shock. I pull on some pants—I've been driving in my underwear—and stand next to a man talking on his cell phone. "Julie, Julie, are you okay?" Julie is my near neighbor, and an acquaintance from around the corner on Tomki Road. The man hands me his cell phone, and I talk to Julie,[2] who got out a little earlier and is now at a motel in Ukiah. She has a double room, and kindly offered to let me share it. It was impossible for either of us to sleep, as we were still in shock from our narrow escape from death.

After that first night at the motel, I was evacuated with the monks from Abhaya-

---

1 Katrena and her husband, Steve Dursteler, risked their lives to wake up all the neighbors in our road, Fisher Lake Drive, off Tomki Road, RV. Steve was distraught because he could not get through the locked gates of the one elderly couple who died in the fire. All other neighbors' lives were saved, thanks to Katrena and Steve, as well as neighbors Frank and Kathy Belford and Dave Kim.
2 Julie is not her real name. I've changed it to protect her privacy.

giri Buddhist Monastery on Tomki Road, to the City of Ten Thousand Buddhas, in Talmage, at the south end of Ukiah.[3] They themselves were on alert to evacuate if the fire spread their way, and we spent the next week or so anxiously watching the spread of the fire on the computer. Fearful of being caught in the flames yet again, I asked one of the nuns about the possibility of CTTB burning down. She gave me the sweetest of looks, and said gently, "But of course it won't." And, of course, it didn't. I will never forget her calm certainty.

So began my journey of homelessness. In the ensuing months, I moved five times. The fire-destroyed property is now derelict, and I'm not sure what I'll do with it. My insurance company, Geico, underwritten by Homesite Insurance Company of California, will pay only about half what it will cost to rebuild. This makes me extremely angry, as Geico spent $1.1 billion dollars on advertising in 2012, which 6.8% of my insurance premiums go to pay for. I've had auto insurance with Geico for twenty-three years without a claim.

A week or so after the fire was finally put out and we were allowed back to see the ruins of our homes, the Buddhist monks came and chanted a blessing at my property. It was a very healing, kind thing they did. (I have been a Theravada Buddhist for nearly thirty years). One of the monks spotted my bronze Buddharupa, lying face-down in the ashes. The ferocity of the fire has burned off his hands, and his face and chest are scorched, but the expression on his face remains serene, compassionate. I have virtually nothing left after the fire, and the things I miss most are precious keepsakes of my husband's—photos, books, clothing. These mementos of our happy marriage cannot be replaced; neither can family heirlooms, antique jewelry, original paintings, coin and stamp collections, and my collection of British horse brasses.

As I write today, August 13, 2018, more fires are raging, part of the Mendocino Complex Fire, which has already consumed 300,000 acres and is still burning. When I ask what we can do to prevent this happening in future, I am told that it is "too expensive" to protect people from these fires. What is a human life worth? Apparently far less than the cost of one US fighter plane or atomic submarine.

Submitted by Anonymous, age seventy-two, widowed six years ago.

3 Neither CTTB nor Abhayagiri Buddhist Monasteries burned. A fireman recounted what happened at Abhayagiri. He was desperately trying to prevent the flames reaching the property, when suddenly the wind changed, and blew the fire back the other way. He was amazed, and said he had never seen something like this happen. All I can think is that someone up there was watching over these places of deep spiritual practice.

Buddharupa statue, owner anonymous. Photo by Laura Herman.

Whiskers the Wildfire Hero
Taffy Montgomery

Shortly after two a.m. October 9, 2017, on the Heart Arrow Ranch, Whiskers, our little eighteen-month-old tuxedo cat, became a hero! The screaming wind battering the house woke me. Outside I could hear patio furniture being blown about, but having lived on the top of this mountain for twenty-five years I was used to high winds. Whiskers figured out it was way more than just wind. I was inclined to go back to sleep, but he would have none of it. Whiskers doesn't have a normal cat voice: He can only squeak, and squeak he did. He jumped up on the bed and squeaked at me, then ran back to the door onto the deck, back and forth until I finally gave in and got out of bed to see if he'd spotted a mouse on the deck.

When I looked out it was like looking into the jaws of hell—fire everywhere; it was even burning in the fields that had burned earlier in the July 2017 Grade Fire. Evacuation was the only hope. I stuffed Whiskers into the bathroom so I could retrieve him after alerting my husband Terry of the dire circumstances. I ran down to the east bedroom where he and Kelly the dog were sound asleep. I turned on the light and yelled at the poor man to get up, get dressed, grab the fire safe, and get out! The fire was coming from the east, and embers driven by 60 mph wind were landing on the house.

There were three boxes of "bottle baby kittens" in the den, terrified by the screaming wind and the smoke alarms that had gone off all over the house. I stuffed the kittens into two boxes, and at that point the alarms stopped and the lights went out. The fire provided sufficient light. Terry came back in yelling, "We have to go." I said, "Take these kittens, I'll get Whiskers." I grabbed his carrier and ran back to my bedroom only to find that the bathroom door had blown open. Where was Whiskers?!

I knew I couldn't look for him, but fortunately I heard him squeaking behind the bathroom door. He didn't resist getting into his carrier. I made the last dash for the truck; fortunately, Terry had opened the garage door before the power had gone. As we backed out of the garage, flames were coming at us through the front.

We were unable to leave, as the fire was raging across the road. For the next half hour we kept moving the truck around, trying to evade the burning embers blown at us. We thought we could take shelter in the steel-covered horse barn, but the wind blew embers into the barn and it exploded.

To add to our concern, our two donkeys and mostly blind horse were in the east paddock. Remarkably, they survived. We weren't allowed to return to the ranch for two days, but we were delighted then to see the three equines, hungry but unharmed.

A footnote to Whiskers: On a very cold day in early November 2015, a woman headed to work in Ukiah saw this little black-and-white bundle of misery crouched in the middle of McNab Ranch Road. She stopped to pick him up and called the Humane Society for Inland Mendocino County. I was at the shelter and told her to get him there as soon as possible. I had little hope when I saw him. His eyes were swollen shut, he couldn't breathe through his nose, and he was stone-cold. Fortunately, a routine of a heating pad, warm subcutaneous fluids, antibiotics, flea control, warm goat milk, and his determination to survive saved him.

I took him home with me at night for several weeks till he finally recovered and was put up for adoption—turnabout is fair play. Who rescued whom? We rescued each other!

Whiskers the Wildfire Hero. Photo by Taffy Montgomery.

We Rescue the Torah
Dan Hibshman

Very early today (October 9, 2017) on KZYX I heard about an extremely serious wild-fire that began late last night and now threatened large parts of Redwood Valley. When Leslie was ready for coffee around six, I told her she'd have to postpone her plan to go to Willits for acupuncture that afternoon, because Highway 101 was closed. At the same time, even bigger and therefore worse fires burned in Napa Valley and Santa Rosa, destroying buildings and forcing evacuations. This was news we first learned when Leslie's older son, Keith, called from his home in Sonoma County, and later so did his ex-wife, Jo, who had their daughter, Kayleigh, and Jo's dogs ready to leave home on a moment's notice. We turned on a Bay Area TV station, which mentioned Mendocino but provided news and images almost entirely of devastation in Napa and Sonoma.

Amidst all these emergencies, I had a strong feeling that the shul of congregation Kol HaEmek, to which I belong and which is located in Redwood Valley, might be in danger. I called Carol Rosenberg and was the first to inform her about everything going on. I asked her who might possibly go to the shul to check on it. She thought of David and Linda Koppel and Louisa Aronow, all of whom live in Redwood Valley and, like Carol (who lives near us here in Ukiah), are active members of the congregation. She tried to call, but couldn't reach any of them, so it came to pass that Leslie and I, with Leslie's dog, Sam, and the key Carol gave us, drove to Redwood Valley to do it ourselves.

Far beyond any devotion to Judaism that I ever exhibit via regular attendance at services or observance of rituals, I was genuinely concerned about the fate of Kol HaEmek's Torah, an authentic relic of the Holocaust. As opposed to unconflicted religious belief and veneration for the written contents of every Torah, the prompting I felt from deep within me to rescue this one had everything to do with its history.

When Kol HaEmek came into existence as a new congregation in Mendocino County, created sometime in the 1980s by otherwise unaffiliated rural Jews, it had no Torah. (At the time it had no shul either.) Someone in the leadership of the group learned that it would be possible to obtain a Torah from a profoundly important source, and here is where that history enters. Apparently, Hitler and the Nazis, not content to exterminate the Jews of Europe, intended to create a "Museum of an Extinct People" in which, among other artifacts, would be displayed Torahs confiscated from synagogues all over the continent. We know, despite the barbaric murder of millions, that no such museum ever came into existence. Instead, after the war a collection of hundreds, perhaps thousands, of Torahs was assembled in London, where they came to be known as the Westminster Torahs. The people responsible for saving and gathering them announced that the relics were available as gifts to other Jewish congregations around the world, and in the course of time Kol HaEmek received a Torah that had once been the beloved possession of a synagogue in Pisek, Czechoslovakia.

For me there may be mixed into this some element of the special affection I feel for what is now the Czech Republic: Because of its films and literature; its revolution led by the playwright Havel; its beautiful capital, Prague, which Leslie and I visited in 1996; and, paradoxically, a grand mal seizure and its aftermath, which I experienced in a smaller Czech city a few days later. Even were it not for these personal affinities, I believe I would still deeply honor Kol HaEmek's Torah as an extraordinary survivor.

Now, anticipating that we'd be carrying the Torah back with us and that it would not fit with Leslie, Sam, and me in the cab of my little pickup, I had fetched our blue tarp and weighted it down in the truck bed with a few old bricks Leslie had collected from somewhere for an eventual landscaping project. We were soon on our way north on Highway 101, but the dire conditions of the fire posed a fundamental question of how—and whether—we'd get where we were trying to go. After so many years of living in inland Mendocino County, I've long known the fundamentals of local navigation, but the present circumstances made those basics unfamiliar, and I debated furiously whether to exit at Calpella or Highway 20 rather than go on as usual to the West Road exit—perhaps only to discover I couldn't get that far or that it was closed. I was correct when I predicted to Leslie that we would soon see an electronic roadside message advising northbound traffic of some kind of closure ahead, but I chose to push on and find out first-hand whether the West Road exit was still open.

All the while we were getting closer to a thick, ominous, brown-gray cloud of smoke that hung, and at this early stage of the fire was expanding, over Redwood Valley.

The fact that the West Road exit was open validated for a moment my decision to go that far north, but as soon as we climbed to the end of the off-ramp we could see that we wouldn't be able to go any farther. A California Highway Patrol car was positioned in the middle of the road we would normally have taken, with lots more cars and trucks parked and several dozen people standing uneasily nearby. We found a narrow spot to park and began walking toward the CHP vehicle. To my surprise, no one objected to our walking past it and then on to the intersection of West Road and School Way. There, dozens more people stood watching the deputy sheriff and a couple of other uniformed men who seemed to be in charge.

I'd said to Leslie when we walked from the first checkpoint to this one, "You do the talking." Now she approached the fresh-faced deputy and launched into an explanation/request regarding what we wanted to do. He listened to her rapid account of the Torah's poignant history, but without hesitation obeyed the instruction he'd been given: deny everyone access to beyond where he and his Mendocino County Sheriff patrol car were standing.

Briefly, softly, I pleaded that we wanted to go less than a hundred yards up West Road, to a point adjacent to a speed-limit sign we could easily see, in order to get to the shul, but there was no denying the reasonableness of what he was telling us: "All these people want to go out there for something." He did say we could go to the fire department, in "downtown" Redwood Valley, which I knew was less than half a mile away, and ask the command center there to provide us an escort to our destination. I considered this, but somehow knew that for us it was the wrong way to go.

Then a guy in a green T-shirt—not in any uniform, in other words, but standing nonetheless as one of the cluster of people with the deputy—spoke to us a little outside the hearing of the others. He suggested what I already partly knew to be true: That Leslie and Sam and I could walk up a long driveway from School Way to its other end, which would put us right behind the shul. Doing that would probably mean trespassing, I realized, but it would be out of sight of the deputy, who had far more important matters on his mind. Though I had driven past those houses on School Way many times, I'd never studied them individually. Now, though, as we (Sam on Leslie's leash) walked away from the roadblock, I could quickly see what the man in the green tee meant—a long driveway extended at least as far back as the rear of the shul.

Leslie suggested I knock on the front door of the closest house, so I did, rapping its knocker a distinct three times. Nobody answered. We walked up the driveway, the big gray gym of Eagle Peak School easily visible the whole way. (In totally pleasant past times we'd gone there many times to watch Audrey, my granddaughter, play basketball.) We were alert to the possibility that at any moment someone might call out, perhaps hostilely, to ask what we were doing, but no one did, and in a short time we were adjacent to Kol HaEmek. Though its front, on West Road, was more familiar, I easily recognized this back side: the deck I once contributed some of my labor to build and, on and above it, the sukkah.

To get to our destination we had to climb over a fence whose wire strands hung on ceramic knobs attached to wooden posts several feet apart. Leslie went first, and I kept Sam from getting tangled in either the fence or the wild oats growing beneath and around it; fortunately, there was a lot of slack in the wire, and Leslie had no difficulty getting over. I picked up Sam, handed him across to her, then managed to get over myself.

We weren't there yet, but my best recollection said we simply needed to find one more driveway. This one was an extension of the shul's own entrance from West Road, and as recently as the sukkah day I had seen, not for the first time, that it led—unblocked—to a neighboring property where a big recreational vehicle was parked. Having climbed over the fence, I could see that same RV close by, and in no time we were on Kol HaEmek's own property.

There was every reason to move quickly. We went to the front and used the key to open the door. The ark containing the Torah, a tall, exotic wooden cabinet built for that purpose, stood in a corner of the not very large room. I walked directly to it and opened its double doors. For the briefest instant I wondered if I should make a gesture, maybe offer a prayer of some kind, to affirm what we were doing, but no idea of what to do other than lift the Torah out of the ark occurred to me.

The Torah is the first five books of the Bible, known also as the Five Books of Moses. It is hand-lettered in Hebrew, written on one long scroll of parchment that is wound around two wooden poles. No doubt some other congregations' are much fancier, but each of the poles holding Kol HaEmek's is basically a narrow rod, unadorned at the bottom and with a simple finial at the top. Traditional Jewish practice, I'd learned long after my boyhood, is to reread the entire Torah over the course of every year, dividing it into fifty-two portions; the poles are used to advance the scroll weekly just to the next portion, and at the end of that non-Christian year there's a special holiday at which time the scroll is entirely rewound to its beginning.

But now, with the Torah wrapped in a multicolored velvet "dress," the object I lifted out of the ark appeared to be not a scroll at all, just the two poles, in view both at the unclosed bottom of that covering and in their extension through two holes sewn in the top. A silver pointer, used in reading the Torah so as to prevent human hands from touching it directly, was draped on a delicate chain around the tops of the poles. I lifted the chain and handed it to Leslie, then hefted the Torah into my upper arms, and after she locked the door we left.

I recall that her cautious sense of the way to proceed was to go back the way we'd come. Besides not wanting to reclimb that fence, though, I felt very confident we should walk openly along West Road, past the roadblock and to the truck. As we did this, I was aware not only of the scene we were approaching but also of the terrible fire behind us. Simultaneously there was the dire anxiety of people restrained from going home, and the quiet importance of our now leaving Redwood Valley.

I figured the deputy probably noticed the three of us plus the addition of the object I was carrying, but I also figured that what we'd done hardly rose to the level of lawbreaking; he had far more on his mind than to challenge our leaving the area that a few minutes earlier he hadn't allowed us to enter. I noticed caps on two men standing near him. One read NATIONAL RIFLE ASSOCIATION, the other WARDEN, and I figured he was with Fish and Game. As we passed by I instinctively said, "Thank you" to the latter. "I didn't do anything," he solemnly replied.

The load in my arms began to feel heavier. I remembered times in the past when I'd been invited to hold this Torah during a Kol Nidre service but politely declined, citing a problem in my back. In fact I'd been having that same sort of problem recently and had gone to the shul counting on adrenaline to overcome any strain that might arise. For most of the walk I'd been gratified to note how relatively light the Torah felt, despite my carrying it almost entirely with my upper body—exactly what, in order to avoid back injury, people are commonly advised not to do. Now near the end of the walk, between the roadblock and the CHP vehicle, I needed to shift the Torah's weight somehow. First I bent my knees and then, when I straightened up, I made the poles more horizontal, which for the final yards made them easier to carry.

I asked Leslie to go ahead and open the tarp. Close to the pickup we encountered the man in the green T-shirt, who was joyously glad to see our success: "God bless you!" he called out and gave us a wonderful hug. I was certain he wasn't Jewish, which mattered not at all.

My Story
Cindi Goldberg

A dark night began when the phone rang. I heard the frantic voice of my sister telling me she and her family were coming over, as they had to evacuate. I was clueless as to what she meant, as all was very calm on my side of town. I switched on our lights all over, inside and outside the house, and began to prepare blankets and makeshift bedding. Then, five people and four cars appeared in our driveway. This was the beginning of their losses (four homes, one kitten, and a business truck) and all of our sorrows, loss, and resiliency.

Willts Strong. Tough times don't last, tough people do. Photo by Ree Slocum.

That night, my heart felt that this disaster took all our lives into another world. My family stayed with my husband and me till they were given a roomier home in Lake County to stay in. This was two seniors, plus their daughter, her partner, and their two-year-old child. Tears, disbelief, sleepless nights, and thoughts of where and how to begin anew overwhelmed everyone. The bonding of their love and knowing they'd made it to our house alive kept them going. Phone calls, drives to Lake County to help in any way possible, crying, holding each other, taking walks, cooking meals, sharing, and doing whatever was necessary became their everyday existence.

Over this one-year period, since the fire they've moved to two homes and settled in a rental in Willits, continually dealing with all the insurance claims and endless paperwork, attending fire-victim meetings, and learning how and where to start all over. I saw how they, as a family, lived together again and how the grace, caring, support, giving, and love of the Redwood Valley community and beyond came to their aid as a truly helping community. It gave me faith and belief in the whole of Mendocino County that they came to rescue and renew my family. I had a change of heart and attitude; I learned to value the importance of letting go of personal things and accept what I now knew as the new normal in all our lives. I treasure each day I'm with my loved ones, and understand what my sister means when she says no one can fully get it, especially when people say that having insurance will cover it. Their resilience has taken its toll in lots of ways, but when there is the joy, laughter, and play of a three-year-old in the everyday picture... that makes each day a new beginning. There have been renewed friendships, trips to the beach, and clearing of their land; soon there will bea manufactured home to move into, and this coming October we will give thanks and make blessings.

The last glimpse of the pine trees. Photos by Cassie Taaning.

Photos by Cassie Taaning.

Regrowth on a burned tree. Photo by Cassie Taaning.

Awakening to Wildfire
Tamara Frey

Where to begin with the insanity of my life? When the worst firestorm in US history roared through our lives, our homes, our backcountry road in the middle of the night.

My daughter glanced back, eyes sweeping her room, drawers askew, and I thought, I'll clean up when we get back—but there was no going back. Ever. No home, no messy bedroom, no beloved dog, nothing—just a scattering of gray toxic rubble.

The wildfires that raged through our lives that night, destroying all homes, sheds, cabins, barns, and buildings within a five-mile radius except for one lone lucky home where the wind must have changed at the last instant, was a rare force of nature. Almost nothing could survive it. People talk of when "all hell breaks loose." Imagine what that would look like. Now we know.

The fires were a freak of nature, they say, and that lone neighbor whose home wasn't razed feels survivor's guilt for even having a home to return to. I tell them to feel blessed, incredibly blessed, that they have a home. A girlfriend who didn't like her home now loves it, and is putting time and energy into it, so grateful that she still has a home.

For me, the adventure called life began on May 14, 1955 at four a.m. I pushed

Helicopter dipping water from the Eel River. Photo by Manya Wik.

forth, gazed unblinkingly into my father's eyes, grabbed his little finger with a strong, stubborn grip, and would not let go. I was a Taurus, ready to charge through life and bulldoze ahead, an attitude that has served me well, especially during critical times when the words of my beloved mother pour forth like a fountainhead: "Persevere, honey, all we can do is persevere." This is one of those times when her words are a gentle reminder that we can choose to either lie in a heap and howl or get up, brush off the soot and ashes, and march into the glowing horizon as best we can.

Gone my home of twenty-five years, my cozy nest, my cluttered mess, gone in one fell swoop, one raging blaze. All of it gone; yet in my mind's eye it is still there, in full bloom and sparkling color, and always will be. A lifetime exists in a home, and many lives went up in smoke that night, devoured by the dragon's fiery breath. Nine lives were lost in our area alone. Such incomprehensible tragedy. Things that take a lifetime to accomplish: raise three children, gather precious photos, artwork, and artifacts from around the world; my best culinary equipment, catering pots, pans, chef's knives, gone. All my culinary research: recipes, menus, anecdotes from the past fifty years, gone. A lifetime of experience and learning exists in a home. A lifetime of love and loss and joy and sorrow exists in a home. All that is tangible in those precious experiences that occur in a home went up in flames.

Documentation no longer exists. The things that are irreplaceable no longer exist. After losing everything, my eldest son dropped his phone in the dog's water bowl and lost that too. "I feel as if my past is being erased!" he lamented. In the end

Los Angeles firefighters from Inglewood Station #173 look across to the new firebreak. Photo by Manya Wik.

Fire flares on a ridge above Potter Valley. Photo by Manya Wik.

all we have are the cherished memories, which will always be within.

Losing one's home is a profound experience and an extreme adventure. One's entire perspective changes. At first all sense of belonging is lost and attachment no longer exists. A friend admired a skirt I was wearing recently, so I took it off and gave it to her. One can live a lifetime in just three weeks, and in a strange way a lifetime did go by in the month of October 2017. The phone rang at 12:30 a.m. on October 9, 2017. I didn't hear a thing. Thank goodness we had a landline. We turned off our cell phones at night. Now, in the aftermath, I'm afraid to turn off my cell phone—ever.

My daughter, Maria, woke up to the sound of a friend leaving a message on our phone. She ignored it for a second, thinking, Well, I have to pee anyway. She got up, went to the bathroom, and listened to the message from a girlfriend up the valley who said there was a fire coming our way and we might want to check it out.

Maria walked outside and saw flames through the trees. Her whole body began to tremble and she came and woke me, her heart pounding.

I remember falling asleep that night to an incredible wind outside thinking, Wow! If a tree falls on us, will the house be okay? Will we be safe?

The next thing I knew, my daughter's silhouette was framed in my doorway, the living-room light behind her. She didn't know how to tell me what was happening. "Mom," she said, fear in her voice. "There's a fire outside."

I scrambled out of peaceful slumber, hurried outside and, from our porch, saw along the eastern hills a huge wall of smoke with brilliant dancing flames that roared like a jet engine at full throttle. An orange full moon hovered over this surreal scene, the same color as the flames.

"It didn't look real," my daughter said. "It looked like an intense painting that I was staring at."

In the south there was another fire coming our way. I think the two fires met in our area, which now looked like a bomb had dropped—an area of spectacular destruction and desecration.

I froze, and sized up the situation. I kept blinking my sleepy eyes. It was hard to comprehend what I was seeing. Holy shit! Holy crap! Holy fuck! All the world's cuss words couldn't do it justice. Then a sense of panicked urgency set in, and I was in extreme flight mode. Two deadly armies were advancing toward us at an alarming rate. I blocked out everything but a laser-like focus on getting to the elders: to get my ninety-three-year-old mother and eighty-seven-year-old uncle the hell out of there, as hell was fast approaching.

I woke everyone up saying, "There's a fire, we have to get out of here now." That was it, that was all that was said.

I grabbed the smaller animals, left the larger ones—two big labs. I didn't reason, couldn't think, just did what I could. I regret that. They'll run, I thought. They'll be okay.

An hour and a half later, at 3 a.m., one returned: Appearing out of the mountaintop darkness, Harley, smelling of smoke, strode toward a man and his family who were ready to evacuate. They'd had more time—time to think, time to reason. I thank that man every day for taking Harley with them that night. With four dogs, four adults, and a pile of people's belongings in my car, there wasn't room for the big beasts.

Looking back, we could have made it work. We could have sat on top of each other. In the moment, though, there was no rational thought; there was only reaction, and when I got far enough away with the elders to feel safe, I tried to reach people to get the big dogs. Alas, it was too late. Dakota, Harley's father, disappeared. Losing Dakota has been one of the hardest parts in all of this. We dowsed for him, my girlfriend and I, searched and dowsed for Dakota. There have been five sightings of a large black lab, three of them near where his son was found. He runs away every time, which doesn't sound like him. Who knows? Maybe someday Dakota will find his way home. I pray he's safe and at peace wherever he is now. I'm sorry, Dakota. You didn't deserve that. I panicked and reacted and did not know the magnitude, the massive destruction this fire would leave behind. I didn't know the meaning of the word "firestorm." What happened was unfathomable. I am so sorry. You were such a devoted and loyal friend. I wish I could have been stronger, been able to think more clearly. I loved our swimming days. We loved you.

In a panicked situation such as that, there is a fleeting split-second thought process: "What shall I take?" It is so overwhelming—one wants to take the whole house, one's whole existence: photos, computer, clothes, the kitchen and everything in it, all beloved pets, the whole kit and caboodle. When there's no time, when it's vastly overwhelming in that instant, one takes nothing but the clothes on one's back. No time to think rationally, no time for anything but to just get out of harm's way.

My daughter grabbed her dirty laundry with no idea why. My brother grabbed his wife's jewelry, which I thought was so sweet, and then ripped their computer out of the wall in a mad rush. I grabbed a watermelon. In the days that followed, we enjoyed its sweet juicy wetness as we wandered around, dazed and numb.

After I grasped the meaning of the advancing distant roar, I grabbed the first clothes within reach and got dressed. The phone rang. It was one of my sons. He said "Mom, head north, there's a wall of flame at the end of Tomki." Thank God I could hear him through the static-filled connection—I was so grateful the phone towers hadn't gone down yet. I knew then that my older son and their father would be alerted. I called my youngest brother and, amazingly, he answered. He and his family were sound asleep. They would be safe.

We'd had a fire scare a few months earlier and had all gotten fire hoses, which we laid out with plenty of water pressure. We felt ready! Never did I think that maybe the pump down the way would burn up and that the water would go down or that the electricity would go out. There was nothing—no sirens, no firemen, no help, no water, no electricity, no phones, nothing. We were on our own. There were fifty-four of us on our ranch that night. The men gathered at the end of the driveway to the main house to make sure everyone was called, alerted, and accounted for. They were the last to leave.

One of my brothers, who had a newborn and a three-year-old, couldn't get out. He bulldozed around his home to save it, but they'd waited too long. They hurried back through the burning field and ended up in the warehouse, an insulated metal building full of wine. He was able to put out spot fires around the main house—our childhood home and our mother's house—as the winery burned down around them. They were safe.

I raced over to my mother's house and went into her room where she was sleeping soundly. "Mom, there's a fire. You need to get up and get in the car, now." We ushered her out of there fast. Luckily it was a few minutes before all the electricity cut out.

We ended up at the coast the next morning, where the air was breathable. We then spent the first night at the shelter in Willits. Our bodies were in shock, and we couldn't sleep or eat for days. My brain had short-circuited, and when I'd try to sleep, the flashing fire images would not stop. It was like firecrackers continually going off in my head. I remember not wanting to hear the words "your house is gone." As long as those words weren't spoken there was still a sliver of hope.

A friend called my daughter and told her he'd gone to our land.

"Is our house still there?" she asked.

"No," he said. "Nothing is there, everything's gone."

For a week we had six people, four dogs, and a parrot in our little hotel room. Wandering around in a stupor, I realized I had no underwear or socks but those I'd hastily put on as we fled. The clothes on our backs were all we had—and not even our nicer clothes! The community organized immediately and set up stations throughout the county to distribute free clothing. We are forever grateful for that. In one of the piles, I found a long white skirt from India that had little round metal mirrors all over it. Shortly after the fires, I wore it on Halloween and went as "a ray of hope."

They call us fire victims, but we are fire survivors.

I find myself thinking of how the fire came. Which part of my home went up

Backfire burning above Cape Horn Dam, Potter Valley. Photo by Manya Wik.

first? Did the house fill with smoke so thick you couldn't cut it with a knife? Did it slam into the south side of the house, engulfing it all suddenly and completely like a raging evil force, a witch's cauldron gone mad? It broke down my door with a force that razed twelve homes and seven structures on our ranch alone that night, and we were the lucky ones—we made it out alive.

Did the flames eat my photos first? Photos of my smiling cherub babies? Did it devour in an instant with its dragon breath photos of my young boys dressed as Batman, their innocent smiles melting? Did my chef's knives curl and melt, dancing in the flames?

How did dear Mr. Fish go? Did his tank seals melt first, sending him sprawling into the steamy abyss, gulping and convulsing? Did the water douse any flames? Did the water in his tank boil him first? I can see him frantically darting back and forth, till the glass gave way, spilling him forth. We'd had him six years. He was huge! I used to wonder, how long does a dollar fish live? The only living thing left in the darkened house as the power and water and phone lines all burned in the wall of fire and smoke, he lived in water and died by fire.

My girlfriend who lives down the valley noticed an evil wind whipping through her backyard that night, and felt a destructive force in the air. It chilled her to the bone. She felt a bad omen, felt that something terrible was brewing. It felt like a hurricane and sounded like a thousand lions roaring, rattled her entire barn as if it were getting ready to take off.

My life has changed dramatically over the last six weeks. I want my house back, I want my dog back, I want my garden back. I want it all back, yet we're forced

Firefighter using a drip torch for backfiring. Photo by Ole Wik.

forward—if you can call it that. Forward into what? There's an emptiness, a feeling of nothing to grab on to. Nothing made sense anymore. One's hogar, or hearth, is an anchor. I always felt so relieved to get home, to just "be" at home, even though I needed to do major decluttering and was always working on it! The universe took care of that for me, but did it have to be such an extreme decluttering? I've been thinking: What is the universe trying to tell me? But this catastrophe happened to so many of us that the universe isn't really trying to tell any of us anything. It just is what it is. Nothing more. My statues survived, Quan Yin, Ganesha, a bit charred but standing and sitting still. It felt like peace within the conflagration. Quan Yin— Goddess of compassion, a healing balm in this insanity called life.

I loved driving up my driveway and seeing my dogs hopping about as they welcomed me home. I'd feel the hard work and long trips of cooking and feeding people melt away, and a softening would occur, a settling in once again. Getting things done, planting winter greens or spring and summer gardens, the cycle of the seasons; readying woodpiles and kindling for winter—we were so ready this year. My daughter had worked hard; she'd meticulously chopped kindling to assure the upcoming winter's warmth, but it all just turned into more fuel for the raging dragon. Now our lives will be forever defined by "before the fires" and "after the fires."

Life goes on, and like the phoenix we rise from these ashes, a bit "dented" as one dear friend put it, yet perhaps stronger for it. We certainly don't feel stronger; we feel stunned, numbed, and forever changed. We fall apart completely and easily. It wells up, that stirring of the blood in the pit of the belly, and rises up like a great, uncontrollable, hot wave. And once again we are aflame.

My cat, Tigre, appeared at our charred homesite three weeks after the fires. With burned paws and singed whiskers, he stumbled back to the only home he's ever known and miraculously was able to survive. He was skin and bones and ate voraciously. He had a new little home, a dog igloo with a wool blanket. He felt lonely, I could tell, but was gaining strength. He howled his misery, trying to tell us his woeful tale of what he must have gone through. He was always an outdoor cat, more wild than tame, and somewhat of a bully. He was much tamer now, needing the contact of human warmth. He and Dakota had been buddies. Tigre used to wrap his tail around Dakota's face. I know they were somehow together that fateful night and helped each other as best they could, the instinct to survive pushing them both forward. Tigre has since disappeared again. I hope someday he'll come home. It feels like we've talked for a lifetime about the fires, and still it feels like it will take more than a lifetime to process it all. It will never be extinguished.

I've heard that some people went into swimming pools as the fires raged around them and, six hours later, emerged amongst the ruin. Some did not survive. They are the fire victims. I heard that a legally blind man walked to the nearby creek bed when he realized he wouldn't be able to get out in time, and buried himself in the dirt and rocks. The fire swept over him and he stumbled safely away afterward.

A neighbor's bridge over the wide creek bed was aflame. They couldn't get out, but were able to get to the field behind the fire and watch as their home and out-buildings and cars burned all around them.

Another friend awoke to fire blasting through his window. Able to run to his car, he could barely drive through the flames on his precarious road; winding along the hill, he had to stop and wait for the smoke to clear enough as the car got hotter and hotter. He made it to the other side of the fire and sat in the meadow, watching his home as it was devoured by the beast. His barn survived, and he holed up in it for four days, stuck there, frozen blueberries from his slowly defrosting freezer his only provisions.

A neighbor awoke to the sound of explosions and raced down her driveway to find a wall of flame. She and another neighbor and her children had to hike up the mountain to escape in the middle of the night. My sons lived at the end of her driveway, and in his house one of them had $500 worth of the biggest, baddest firecrackers one could buy; I'd gotten them for him a month earlier on the way back from Burning Man. I like to think that the sound of those firecrackers igniting all at once woke people up.

Last night, as I drove back to where I now live, I automatically headed home, toward my home that is still there only in my mind's eye. I just started weeping. "I want to go home! I want to go home!" I howled to the universe. We are disoriented and adrift, all just hanging on by our fingernails. Nothing makes sense anymore. I can't get my bearings. And we are the lucky ones.

My brother up the way stayed as long as he possibly could, hosing down his house, trying to save the hand-hewn home he'd built for his budding family a year ago. When the 200-foot-high flames engulfed my home across the field, and the water went down, and the firestorm dragon started to whip across his meadow, he felt himself panic as he jumped on his four-wheeler and headed north into the woods.

Debating whether to jump into the pond nearby or keep heading north, he calmed himself and went north.

Some of the men, brothers, sons, and nephews, were able to go in the back way before the blockade. They holed up in the few dwellings in the Northern Ranch that survived the first onslaught. Another brother had left a pump in his field, trying desperately to get water from the pond nearby to his home after the water went down. They found that pump a few days later, and were able to keep the few northern buildings from burning as the fire continued and burning trees fell and rolled down the hillside. They were on a 24-hour watch, and by pumping water from the old swimming pool they were able to save those dwellings. They could not leave—if they did, they wouldn't have been allowed back in. A few days later, when we were allowed in, we refreshed their provisions. They had a continuous pot of soup, just kept throwing into it anything they could find. There was no water or electricity. It was a siege.

I had a friend, Zephaniah, camping in my yard and helping me on my land at the time. After the fires someone found a page of the Bible in the rubble, burned around the edges. The book of Zephaniah! Quite auspicious. He went back in to help keep the remaining northern dwellings from burning down after the apocalypse.

When we were able to get back in a few days later, we found that my brother's gardens and orchards survived, but none of the surrounding buildings had. My brother's three cows, six sheep, and two pigs had somehow survived, a bit blackened and singed, but they were fine; and one of the pregnant cows had birthed a calf, which calmly dozed on the cooled ash under a burned tree. His name is Sparky Phoenix Firestorm, Blaze for short.

Now I sit in my cozy Tiny House on wheels, my brother's surviving animals outside my window. Baby Blaze romps around the barnyard that these fire-surviving animals brought back to life in the place where we landed. It's a very peaceful place, an idyllic scene surrounded by a barnyard and vineyards. Not a bad life, this new life after the fires, but a very different life.

They say that fire is cleansing, but fire is spectacularly devastating, massive, desecrating, not cleansing at all.

This experience is like being grated raw, down to the bone, exposing one's soul, yet we are the lucky ones—we are alive, and there is much to be grateful for. I know it will take time to feel whole again. I allow myself that time.

I prayed every day: "Please get us to the safety of the rains." I was nestled in a tinderbox, with no defensible space. In the end it wouldn't have mattered. It all fueled the raging beast, though this dragon needed no fuel.

Allowed back in a few days later, we inspected the desecration, the gray toxic rubble that just a few days ago had been our home and our treasured possessions. I dug through my jewelry area and found one burned, twisted, blackened earring. The toilet was shattered. It was unbelievable what the firestorm accomplished. Everything melted, twisting, and writhing. Hubcaps created art as they melted, flowed,

Smoke rising over a blackened firebreak. Photo by Manya Wik.

and cooled. Glass danced in the inferno, artistic beauty emerging.

In the back garden, where the fire beast continued its deadly sojourn, I discovered a perfectly crisp and crunchy Japanese cucumber. We ate it, unable to believe how chance rolls the dice. In stunned disbelief, we munched baked apples off the burned apple trees; they were quite good, actually. The Asian pear tree is the lone survivor. I wonder how long it will take for it to bear fruit again.

The Dylan Thomas poem "The Force that Through the Green Fuse Drives the Flower" comes to mind. We can feel that force so strongly as spring flowers that hadn't bloomed in years are blooming brilliant and so full of life. And the green shoots pushing forth on seemingly dead trees are a miracle to behold.

The first time that my land felt hopeful again was when volunteer sunflowers came up all over in places where none had ever been planted. Their shining yellow heads waving in the breeze felt like peace to our injured souls.

We have felt that force so powerfully in this year since the fires.

I am a chef by trade, and my lifelong culinary research, recipes I'd developed, favorite innovative menus saved, all of it gone. Thirty-four years' worth of research and writings on food, and the cookbook I'd been working on for years, gone.

Losing all the baby pictures of my children caused me a grief that a year later has not subsided. A wellspring of grief that at times I can't control surfaces every time I begin to talk about it. I am searching to understand. I catered for a therapists' workshop recently, and it was the one-year anniversary of the fires. As I shared with one of them about losing all my baby pictures, I completely lost control. I splashed cold water on my face and tried desperately to gain control of the overwhelming grief within, as the rest of the guests were due any moment for lunch. I knew they would understand, but it was no time to lose it. I regained my equilibrium in the nick of time.

We want to have a healing ceremony on the demolished land. For the trees, for the land, for Dakota, for Mr. Fish, for Tigre the cat who survived the fires only to then disappear. My daughter had the brilliant idea to camp there on the land and just spend some time there. We went to the burned-out land, started to cry, and left. Now we don't cry so much when we're there, but we haven't spent much time there since that life-changing night.

Memories of My Home

I loved how the afternoon sun shone into my bedroom windows, right onto my bed; I loved to lie there and read in the sunlight.

I loved how I could open the bedroom double doors at dawn when the wild geese were migrating north or south and their calls echoed through me. I felt so blessed to live on their path.

I loved the hardwood floors in the living-room/kitchen area that came out of an old high-school gymnasium.

I loved the light of the full moon that shone through the skylight above; when I lay in bed I could see the full moon at just the right angle at the right time, illuminating my world in the middle of the night.

I loved the view from the front porch: of the brilliant full moon rising through the trees and over the hill in the east. I would bathe in the moonlight, arms spread wide, soaking up the healing energy.

I loved the quiet of the country that surrounded me, and the peace of the country darkness and fresh cold air at night.

I loved the spring water from the hills above.

And then one night in October it was unseasonably warm and the wind was wild and severe, so severe that as I lay in bed, drifting into slumber, I remember thinking, Wow! What if a tree falls on the house? Will the house be okay? Will we be safe?

Linnea Wik examines knobcone pine seeds released by the heat of the wildfire. Photo by Manya Wik.

Since the Fire...
Amelia Hiseley

The weekend the fire began in early October 2017, I had just celebrated my birthday with family on the coast. It was one of those rare perfect days, unusually warm and clear, that's still etched in my mind. On Sunday, October 8, I was back to work. It was just an ordinary day till the wind started. I walked outside one last time that night to take the dog out to pee. I stood in the front yard as those hot crazy winds whipped through the trees above. The rest of the family had gone to bed. In the dark I could see that while I was inside watching TV, a large limb of the eucalyptus tree had come down and was lying ten feet from the house.

Despite how unsettled I felt, I tried to go to bed around 1 a.m. By 1:30, my eighteen-year-old daughter was next to my bed telling me a friend of mine from Potter Valley was trying to reach us. She said there was a fire that started over the hill in Potter and they were now evacuating. Then, as we started to wake up and assess what was happening, the lights flickered and went out. It must have been closer to 1:45 when we received the emergency alert call. I went outside on the deck just off the master bedroom and noticed the air seemed eerily still. I was able to peer through the trees to the sky above, where a reddish glow stretched across both sides of Redwood Valley, lighting up the entire night. It was hard to tell where the fire came from. I stood in the quiet of the winds, which had calmed, and heard loud booms in the distance. I learned later that those were propane tanks exploding on the other side of the valley.

We didn't waste much time after that. We couldn't find the cat in the dark. I remember the moment that we were loaded up, waiting on the others in the family. I was sitting in the driveway, looking at the shell-shocked expressions on the faces of my three boys in the car, and thinking, We're all here, that's all that matters. It's okay. Stuff is... just stuff. Not thinking clearly at all, I had left behind my purse, and my two middle sons had no shoes. My youngest, then almost four, still recalls being woken up and put in the car, his dad saying, "We have to go, Go, GO!"

Having gotten to know the terrain of this valley far better since the fires happened, and seeing the landscape change, I'm much more aware of my surroundings. We were on the very edge of the fire, where it burned out. The neighborhood sits much farther in, below the rim of the mountains, which are shaped like a boomerang that stretches east and north. Before the fire, I thought they were so far away; afterward I realized how close everything is and how much more of the mountains are now visible after half our yard plus our neighbors' entire property was gone. No more fences.

Those early days when we were evacuated are hazy. I mostly remember fear and heartache over the loss of those who died and the horrific news in Sonoma County. I remember the relief of finding out our house was spared, and I especially remember unwavering hope. The outpouring of compassion and generosity from this community in the face of such loss was simply amazing. I listened for news of my hometown, Santa Rosa, and all they were going through, but my heart was here with Mendocino County all along. Looking back at my Facebook posts, I stumbled on this story I wrote on October 13, 2017:

One of those neighbors is someone I've since gotten to know better. We could

Amee Hiseley
October 13, 2017 · •••

Today we learned the rest of the story about how our home wasn't lost.

There are silent heroes among us. Our neighbors are heroes to us. They stayed behind. I thought they were crazy. And yet so many stories are now being told of the ones who helped others to safety or guarded their "kingdoms" (phrase borrowed from a friend)

We found out today that it wasn't Cal fire that saved our home. We are told they came later to put in the fire break. I'm sure they had their hands full just getting people to safety first.

We learned it was our neighbors James and Kyle who seeing their own home go up in flames, abandoned their efforts to save their garden (grow) & used irrigation water to stop the onslaught of flames headed towards ours. Such bravery, and amazing kindness from neighbors we barely knew!

Only one small structure is burned, the one furthest away from the house- a play house. Flames were just a couple inches on all three sides of a larger shed on the property (one much closer to the house). It is scorched up to a foot around the sides of the pump house and it cut a large path through the back half and continued on to our adjoining neighbor below- Chet Collins. He has been our hero too. Keeping us in the loop, putting out hot spots. These guys are going on little sleep in the last 5 days. Seriously, amazing!

Tonight I met a couple of others at the high school briefing. One whose home is gone & who I -already knew of, and another I didn't know at all, whose home is ok.

I think we are forever changed. I don't think any of us will ever walk down the street and wonder who lives there anymore. "Off the grid" or out on the "country" many of us kept to ourselves. One of them tonight said she'd been there 30 years! I thought I knew some of them from my kids knocking on their doors for cookie sales, or walking the dog with Liam but after this I think we will be beyond just a perfunctory wave as they drive by or a chat about the weather.

Evacuations are being lifted as they "repopulate" places that are untouched first in our valley. Tonight it's actually calmer than I think was expected. Our neighbors to the east, Potter Valley was told they could return too.

So we still wait. And I know Sonoma & Napa county friends are waiting too, for the worst to pass. I pray for favorable or minimal winds for all of you. You are all in my heart 💜

never have known how this fire would transform us. I believe it started that night. I stopped living half a life and thinking things were "just fine" in my current circumstances. I'm living more fully, becoming more of the person I'm meant to be and embracing change. On the anniversary of that night I think about how it is that we all can find hope in the ashes, like the symbolism of the phoenix finding renewal, rebirth, and resurrection.

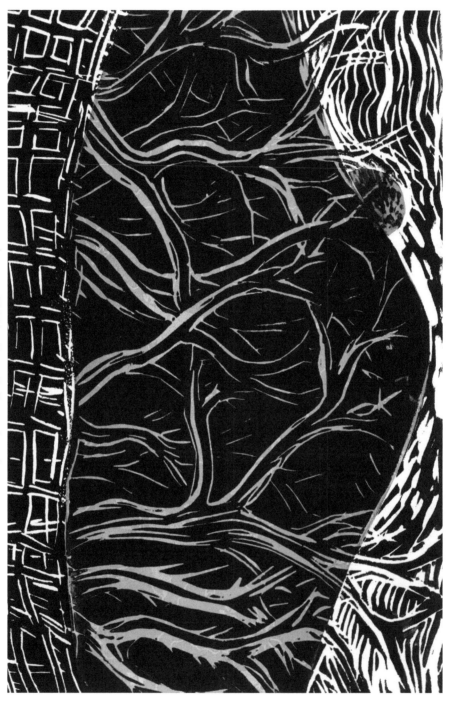

Autumn 2017 by Rose B. Easterbrook.

Poetry and Prose

Speechless
Photograph and Prose by Nori Dolan

Words fell from her lips as flames crowned. Stories of past purpose turned to ash and still she spoke of nothing; however, a sense of gratitude and hope filled her spirit, and she knew the stories would survive in a new and softer landscape.

A Kitchen Darling
In Remembrance of Charlene Foster
Dot Brovarney

A neighbor down the road,
Chef Charle, she called herself.
We call her a Kitchen Darling.

She knitted herself to the J's—
Jane, Joe, Jesse, and Jaelin.
A rare, sweet light
Adopted by all the Frey ladies.

She knitted herself to the land.
A soul blooming with the mountain meadow.
The citrus mandala
In a platter of wildflower moments.

A found poem based on words from interviews with Katrina Frey,
Jaelin Mosscarille, and Jesse Taaning-Sanchez of
Redwood Valley, September 2018.

Wise Fire Poem
Michael Riedell

In this poem I am wise,
I grow bigger than I am, purer.

Like a mountain on fire.
I am the mountain and I am the fire.

And I am the breeze in the afternoon,
And I am the trees.

I work my way out from the center,
And I work my way to ash.

And the wind,
When it picks up again,

Will taste me in its dry mouth.
And the moon,

When it hangs crooked
Like a wry smile and sees the glow

That sends cars careening
To escape it,

That moon,
It will share the wisdom

I can manage in just this poem.
That fire can only take,

So we must learn to give.

A Letter to my Grandmother who Lived in Green Lands
Yvonne Kramer

Grandmother, you lived in green lands

How can you live to see your granddaughter in this dusty, parched land of burrs, wasps, rattlesnakes, and fire?

Grandmother from Limericks' emerald fields, do you lament the choice your son made, to abandon such beauty?

Grandmother from the Alps' flowered meadows, do you lament the choice you made to abandon such grandeur?

But how I wish you could both come to Mendocino in the spring when the creeks are roaring and the fawn lilies grace the banks at Easter.

But please do not come on a hot night in October of lightning and high winds.

Then there is a curse of fire on the land for those who turned their backs on their verdant ancestral lands. In those who replaced the native peoples, who had for thousands of years befriended fire.

Grandmothers, please, come in spirit now to comfort us and bless this ashen land.

Let us walk with the Native grandmothers over the golden hills of Mendocino, with its stubble of green from the first rains.

One Thirty AM
Dot Brovarney

Like an animal,
flames, hot wind carve the hill.

Milled redwood, manzanita, madrone,
charcoal for the Russian River.

Pure creativity,
polisher of rock and stone,
a blank slate—
the beginning of everything.

Found poem: Based on words from an interview with Clint Hudson,
Rancho Mariposa, Tomki Road, December 2017.

Kim's Song
Dot Brovarney

Sky is on fire, singing
sounds tied to rhythm:
bass guitar, banjo, fiddle.
A beat growing—
hand drum, pot drums, congas.

Heartbeat fast
Dark, something dropped.
Catch my breath
didn't have the key
back to house—

Heartbeat fast
Dark, got turned around.
Catch my breath
starting over
Out of gas—

Sky is on fire
Hill ablaze.

What do you take?
Guitar, amp, a piece of land, all
   those trees
too much to carry.

Catch my breath
Starting over.

Create the sounds
I like to play:
bass guitar, banjo, fiddle,
keyboard, some strings.

Get a beat going—
hand drum, pot drums, congas.

I felt like singing,
all those trees felt like singing
offers of spirit and the soul.

Found poem: Based on words from an interview with Kim Monroe,
Rancho Mariposa, Tomki Road, December 2017.

View looking northwest from West Road and Road K around 2 AM.
Photo by Sonya Campbell.

Sonya's grandmother's piano. Photo by Sonya Campbell.

Untitled
Paul Spangenberg

My soulmate came,
Crashing around my room,
Like a wild bird
through the window.
She knocked over all my things…
Jumping around my little cage
My parakeet heart is frantic.
Terrified by her beauty
We rested together…
Come with me
Your dungeon door is now open
and I am standing here waiting
But you have angel wings
and mine are weak from atrophy
I can't
I'm staying here
Looking out my window
at everything on Fire.

While Houses Burned
Yvonne Kramer

While houses burned, I walked outside that morning to see charred pieces of paper
from my neighbors' houses
In Redwood Valley raining down on Greenfield Ranch.
While houses burned, I looked outside our house to see smoke smothering our
canyon.
While houses burned, I called whomever I could reach, but there were those in
Redwood Valley I could not reach.
While houses burned, I listened to KZYX to be calmed by Sheriff Allman's reports.
While houses burned, I packed up photos and art from the walls and random items
to be ready to evacuate.
But still the fire did not come, so I sat in the kitchen for days waiting without strip-
ping the walls of curtains or wetting the roof.
While houses burned, I took up a needle and sewed pillowcases while listening to
KZYX.
While houses burned, I listened to bombers soar overhead, towards Reeves Canyon
to keep the fire from us.
But we did not evacuate, so we offered our small house in town to my son's friend
who had lost his.
After many days I took a walk up our road in the smoke and met a stray black and
white kitty who followed me home.
While houses still smoldered, I pet my new kitty.

Written at workshops led by Poets Laureate
Theresa Whitehill and Michael Riedell

What's Left?
Mary Monroe

Where books once lined a shelf?
Pages of ash, still holding their paper shape.
Where the Japanese Maple once grew from a terracotta pot?
A charred and jagged spear
pointing skyward.
Where children once swung from a tire swing?
A drooping black-trunked oak.
Where summer barbeques and outdoor celebrations provided camaraderie and
delicious food?
There only stands the sad burnt oak.
Where the glass table once stood in front of the bay window
Above the dining table set with hand-made dishes and the indigo tablecloth?
No table! No tablecloth!
No warmth and humor!
Just shards of ceramics and ash.
Pieces of twisted metal.
So much vaporized!
So much gone!
Where is my home?
Where is my life?
Where will I land?

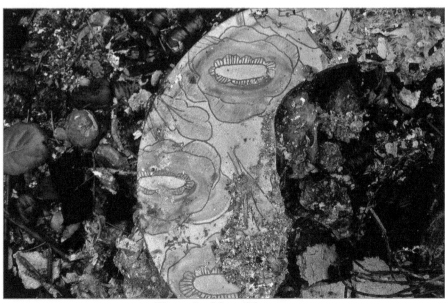

Photo by Mary Monroe.

Ranch Fire
Kayla Wildman

I

a smudge of light gray smoke
rising over a tree-green ridge -
just a small grass fire

away for a few hours…
coming back to
a sky-high billowing plume

a conjunction
of orange: eclipsed moon, Mars,
horizon fire-glow, flames

watching the fire burn
closer, ridge by ridge… then
it dies down for the night

II

suspended between
smooth, flat bands of morning smoke
and looming evacuation

a landscape of smoke
waiting for the fire to wake up -
but online, life just rolls along

watching the plume across the river
and wondering
"Is it time to run for our lives?"

turkey vultures circling -
on the far side,
they dim to ghosts in the smoke

III

walking down the mountain–
the clouds of hell disappear
behind the ridge

our two tiny burros
evacuated
in a six-horse trailer

beneath the blue-black bottom
of the fire's smoke cloud,
an ash-gray mountain

long after sunset,
a wildfire plume in the east
glows hot pink

IV

turning on my computer–
dreading
the wildfire news

how could a small lick of flame
grow to devour
so many mountains?

watching as
evacuation notices
roll across Lake County

red sun rising
through a pall of wildfire smoke
tinged with survivor's guilt

V
the crescendo
and decrescendo of fire planes
all day long

the throbbing roar
of helicopters flying overhead
buckets dangling

brilliant white crowns
of steam emerging from
smudgy gray smoke plumes

sunset – high overhead
a huge tide of orange smoke
moves west

VI
four thousand firefighters
from
one hundred sixty different places

747 supertanker–
massive silver-white plane
slow motion over the mountains

the cool sunset breeze…
one by one, all the fire planes
going home

one a.m. – in the northeast
the mountain horizon
still glowing orange

VII
driving for miles
with fire engines whizzing past…
losing count…

thinking "At least our fire
isn't as bad as…"
and then it out-burns them all

wishing the hard-worked
heroics of firefighters
could just work miracles

VIII
a firefighter dies…
a painful new landscape
of the heart

now a pall of grief
mixes
with the pall of smoke

the procession of sorrow
moves in slow motion
while the fire leaps ahead

IX
living on the edge
of massive disaster
and waiting – for what?

longing for life
to go back to normal
and realizing
it won't

Water Hunt
Georgina Marie

When finding the roots of water
you have to take a long walk down new roads,
you have to start by getting out of bed.

So I begin.

Wearing a yellow ochre sweater
to match the haze in the air,
torn jeans and ash-laden shoes
to make it obvious that I am walking away from disaster
and walking toward disaster.
Taking the first few steps, all I see is exhaustion.

I see a month's worth of sun-turning-red,
a month of trees turning to charcoal.
What I am looking for is moisture.
A cool drip or two to alleviate the heat of summer,
the heat of death.

It is easier to find than water.
Easier to carry the weight of sad bones
than to find light in nerves,
a glimmer in the legs which take so much effort to move.

To find the roots of water
I have to dig deep.
Deeper than only finding the shallow depth of a few well-known truths.
Truth: my sister's ashes came home first.
Truth: my dog's ashes came home second.
Lie: I am ok.

Because just when I thought I was gaining ground on the grieving
it was time to flee home,
time to see the fire,
time to run.

To move with the pounding of buffalo
rushing down mountainsides,
to walk with the hillside lions also looking for water.
With eyes wide open, I can see flames but
I can't see sky,

I can't see the next day.
But I can choke up a ribcage from crying out,
piercing a water source reserved for moments of turmoil.
That's how you know you've gotten down to the roots,
when gallons of water in internal form
come pouring out.

Things I Didn't Lose in the Fire
Georgina Marie

I am enough fire
not to want to find more fire.
I wear it on my Aries skin,
not needing to look too deep to find the blueprints
of red dragon scales
innate in my being.

But these fires just keep coming,
taking my breath away.
I don't breathe fire flames, I don't need to.
They are already all around me.

How many fires does it take anyway?

So I am coming to terms with the life of the fire.

That it didn't burn the parrot wing on my windowsill,
and I thank its orange spirit for it.
That my own scapula is still in place,
and I send a kiss to the smoke.
That I carried my body away from the fire only to return home
when others didn't,
my canine son one of them.

Here I am
with a loneliness that didn't burn away,
parts of my body intact (the ones that still haven't been touched
by any other kinds of fire or sparks or smoldering wants)
but I am still *here.*

The parrot wing, those blue feathers left at my feet
spared for a reason,
is a tool of a lesson of letting go,
a reminder that it is compassion that fills me
as I think of those who lost their feathers to flames
and gained new wings in other worlds.

Ode to Rick
Paul Spangenberg

When the fire came over the mountain
and blazed down the entire backside
stomping its way through the valley
there was really no place you could hide.
It left us all weary and wonderin'
It made us feel naked inside
But there were no tears I was shedding
Until I heard that Rick Loftus had died.
There is loss you can measure and handle
There is loss you can never find
But some loss makes your eyes start to welling
And some loss makes you break down and cry.

Making a Poem After Fire
Georgina Marie

Mix ash with water
and you have the start of a new foundation

one of woman-made mud and words
to help ease you into the next phase of living

after crawling through soot
and inhaling smoke and ochre

after waving a soft hand as the flames slowly die down
and you live to write about it.

But how to find the words when it feels
as though there aren't any stored down deep in the throat,
when leaving home you had enough time to pack belongings
but not enough space to gather syllables.

A firebreak that stopped the flames from moving farther south.

How to find the words when the mockingbirds have stopped
dropping them at your feet
like they used to do each afternoon before singing a song
of repetition and sunlight -
but they too were fleeing the fire.

What is left to say now.
What is left of the blood-red summer
but a mixing bowl sitting on the broken kitchen table
calling you to toss together pieces of debris
to blend a recipe of water and ash,
to create something new to hold

stirring in what is left behind of coughed up poetics
and tears
and more tears

Photo by Ree Slocum.

and the ingredients you've brought yourself through the years:
blue jewels and red bowls,
lapis lazuli and cedar,
and the remnants of loved ones

first come the ashes of a sister
then the ashes of a dog
now the ashes of a long country road you keep circling to find home again
and the ashes of sweetness

how the act of dying makes you want to grow cold
but you are made of amaranth and bone
and roses and water
and none of this can turn you bitter

and how this mixture becomes clay
a thick soul-paste, tender and gray
to mend open gaps, seething wounds

offering a recipe for continuing,
offering unexpected words,
a poem for comfort.

Fire Redux
Hal Zina Bennett

If fire were love, we might
Save the world with kisses and incredulity.
Kissing with fear unleashed, we embrace,
Are set ablaze, children's 4th of July sparklers
Scattering fire, flaming wilderness unbound.
The sky's blush, a nimbus of orange and red and coral,
Fades to shapeless voids, where not even light escapes.
We don't know what it takes to burn the Earth alive,
But history suggests we're up to the job.
We've grumbled enough complaints to 'waken
The gods of chilled indifference, and know at last
Why love so jealously consumes itself.

On the occasion of the Mendocino Complex Fire,
July 27–August 30, 2018, burning 459,123 acres

Winter
Mary Monroe

A strange and ever-changing landscape
Unexpected beauty
In the crisped leaves atop the oaks
In the blackened trunks
In the startling contrast between
what had turned to ash
and
what had turned to crunchy-looking charcoal
In the unusual contrast between tall, blackened firs and winter's green grass.
In the never-so-clearly-seen curves and twists of Madrones
And Manzanitas.

Sad Dancing Madrone. Photo by Mary Monroe.

Blacks and Whites. Photo by Mary Monroe.

"Oh!! Madrone." Photo by Mary Monroe

Untitled II
Paul Spangenberg

Poetry's just not for me
I could never understand it
But someone who is scholarly
Could probably explain it
Nonetheless...
The wolf that wins is the one you feed,
And every day they battle.
One for love, and one for greed
The mystery's unraveled.
Now, I can fix most broken things
If the wolf in me allows it
Learned to fly on broken wings
With not much in my pocket.
The birds have all come back today,
They flew before the fire.
And with them, brought much needed rain
To quench the wolf's desire
Now I can post this on the Internet
or leave it for the waitress
The wolf in you
The one you let
Will be the one who reads this.

Haiku
Cathy Monroe

wildfire survivors
midwinter brings butterflies
grace filled mourning cloaks

fire recovery
narrow backroad traffic snarling
dump trucks rumble by

FEMA street sweepers
Redwood Valley novelty
roads need scrubbing

monstrous jaws grab
rubble chunks of once homes
clearing them away

wildfire clears thick thatch
dormant wildflowers emerge
springing abundant

scaffold of burned limbs
morning glory vines upward
bright bloom on dead oak

tall timber spires
an illusion of forest
only skeletons

Haiku Set
Poems and photos by Cathy Monroe

garden shed jumble
fire's inspiration for
new art pieces

in FEMA work zone
makeshift leash of warning tape
danger dog

crumpled stucco walls
home flattened to wide view
fire swept flower pots

look what the fire brought
tiny owls peering out from
the owl's clover

firestorm's molten rain
barn's aluminum roof flakes
speckling foundation

Evolving
Vivian Sotomayor Power

The longing for our lost things,
Is eclipsed by human need,
By necessity.

The strength of the human spirit
With abundance fills the void
Of the nothing.

The beauty that surrounds us
Lightens our soul, which in due course
Returns to the endeavor of art.

The Shudda Wudda Tree
Jaelin Mosscarille

Abeja said "That is a Jaye tree! I see that tree in lots of Jaye's paintings."
It was a tall gnarly wonderfully outreaching and pulling back tree.
Maybe 20 to 30 feet high it looked as if it had been a wild thing in its youth and now time, experience and natural disaster had shaped it into its current incarnation.
Going every which way and then some. Now it was a charred stump hollowed by the burning embers that continued to smolder even after our attempts to squelch the flames and beat the coals with shovels, sticks and boots.

I ought to have painted her. Never did I like being told what I should paint. I could have given her a proper memorial.

Painting
Poem and Painting by Mary Monroe

Darkness, purple, indigo, deep green…
Crowned with orange, yellow, red, magenta, moving, swirling colors
For days, for weeks
Just laying down color with my brush
Just colors, fire colors, flame colors
Wet on wet, covering an entire page, allowing colors to mingle
Sculpting colors into swirls and curves and points.
One page spoke to me
What is it saying?
What will help to keep me strong?
PAINT ME! Called the Wedge-Tailed Eagle
I will be your phoenix!

Recovery
Mary Monroe

I have found that
RECOVERY
Is an all-encompassing term
And
It comes
Step
by
step . . . .

Beau's Fire Story
Poem and drawing by Beau Decker

This is a poem, about a boy named Beau Decker, I'm five.

Who used to live in: Redwood Valley

Who didn't: See the fire when we left that night. I'm glad I didn't.

Whose house had: A pond, geese, catching fish,
splashing in puddles, a play set, and the big oak tree with the swing.

Who saved: My blanket and my bear. And our dogs, Darby and Cleo.

Who stayed with: Our neighbor, Larry
and then with Nana,
and then a cabin,
Until we moved to our new home,
and Luke and I didn't have to share a bed anymore.

Who misses: My home, the red jeep that I could drive, the geese,
and my Superman Super Shooter.

Who is scared of: Our house burning down again

Who is glad that: Mom and Dad saved me

Who loves: Space and Legos

Who hates: Scrambled eggs and naps

Who dreams of: Being a rock star

Who likes his new home, because:
My family lives here. And my Lego Star Destroyer.

Who is now: A Kindergartner!

Beau's picture.

Burning Ridge. Painting by Jaelin Mosscarille.

Interviews and Articles

Mendocino County Sheriff Tom Allman's Story
Written by Ree Slocum

In 1999, acting Lieutenant Sheriff Tom Allman volunteered to be a "Civilian Peace Keeper" for a year in Kosovo, Yugoslavia. After rigorous interview processes he was chosen as one of 400 police officers from the United States to be there for twelve months to help keep the peace between the Serbs and Albanians. Tom of course bonded with some of the other men and, in April 2017, their first reunion was set up in Las Vegas for the weekend of October 6 and 7. The Allmans planned on flying home on Oct. 8.

While people fled their homes in the at first sleepy and then terrifying wee hours of Monday morning, the Allmans were awakened by phone in their Vegas motel room with the news that Potter and Redwood Valleys were on fire. They flew into action. "My phone started ringin' at one in the morning, so I found out immediately what was happening. My wife was on the Internet. She changed our flights. We got to the airport by six or seven in the morning. Alaska Airlines understood. What happened was that the 101 was closed in Santa Rosa. Closed because of the fires there, and now I had to figure out how to get up to Ukiah. I rented a car in San Francisco. Before I left Vegas I called a friend of mine who lives in Little River and has an airplane. I said, 'Can you meet me in Petaluma?' He said, 'Yeah!' He was going to be there by ten, so we landed at SFO at 8:30 or 9. I got a rental car and in five minutes I was out of there 'cause we had only carry-ons. We got in our rental car and drove to Petaluma Airport. There's no rental car agency there. It's Sunday, and the manager happens to be there because of all the fires. I walked in, gave him my business card, and said, 'You don't know me. I don't know you. Here are the keys to that car out there. If you could try to get it back to the Enterprise in Santa Rosa, I'd really appreciate it!' The airplane was waiting for us. We walked out, got on the plane, and flew to Ukiah.

When the sheriff first got the emergency call in his Las Vegas hotel room he remembers: "I thought somebody was totally exaggerating... what was the real magnitude of this fire? I'll tell you when it sunk in: when we got in the airplane in Petaluma. In the airport nobody was talkin' about Mendocino County. It was all about Santa Rosa and Napa. Once we got in the plane in Petaluma and got above the smoke, it's like ten or 10:30 in the morning, it hit me: "Oh, my God!" When you fly over Kmart and it's gone you go, "What?!" Then you see all those empty houses. We didn't see a lot because of all the smoke, but when the plane went below the inversion layer, you go, "Oh, my God...it's crazy!"

In the private plane, Sheriff Allman was able to use his cell phone and call headquarters in Ukiah to get someone to pick them up from the airport and take him to the Emergency Operations Center in the Mendocino County Sheriff's Complex. His wife stayed with friends in Ukiah. When he was picked up the sheriff said to the driver, "Tell me what's goin' on?" He was up to speed and told me everything he knew. When I walked into the command center it was already set up and going.

I give credit to a woman named Janelle Rau. She works for Carmel Angelo, and she was the one who came in early Monday morning and set it up.

The command center is basically a meeting room with small cabinets in the wall. When they're unlocked and opened, each has its own computer, phone, and stack of supplies. The building also has its own generator so they're ready to go at a moment's notice.

They've trained for a variety of emergencies, but, according to Sheriff Allman, "Not of the magnitude of this fire! How can you train for this?" I walked in, and Janelle took me outside and gave me the genuine lowdown: "This is what we think we have." Because no one knew what we had. We didn't know how many deaths, how many houses we'd lost, how many fire engines were out there, and so forth.

"This is gonna sound cold but let me say it: Running a disaster is like running a business during really tough times. Make a decision and move on. And the decisions we made? Most of them were really good ones. You never want to be good at a disaster, because that means you've been through a lot of them, but I think we were pretty good. I think our deputies had the Nomex [fire-retardant clothes], we had Reverse 911, and we started NIXLE, so we could get any emergency broadcast the sheriff's department put out. So if it's a tsunami you'll get the alert."

"Our emergency operations center was set up within an hour. CAL FIRE was doin' their job and the sheriffs were doing evacuations. I was satisfied with our response and how we were dealing with it. The decisions that could've been improved upon? We're improving them."

"We knew—and this is crucial—that Laughlin Peak, which is our communications tower between Potter and Redwood Valleys and Willits was lost." The sheriff breathed deeply and sighed. "Ugh! It was one of these 'Oh, no!' situations, because that meant Willits [isolated because of the road closing] had no hard line, no 911, no cell line, no Internet!"

People were starting to arrive at Ukiah Valley Medical Center with burns and other injuries, and the hospital was running out of supplies. Communications were down with Howard Memorial Hospital in Willits, and Lake and Sonoma County hospitals were filled with their own fire-survivor injuries. There was nowhere to turn immediately for more supplies.

Directly related to that problem: a few years ago Sheriff Allman and district attorney David Eyster decided to purchase four satellite phones in case of emergencies in which communications were lost, as during this fire. There was a satellite phone in Howard Hospital in Willits, at the UVMC in Ukiah, the Redwood Valley Fire Station, and the command center. The sheriff, however, explained a glitch in this emergency plan, "When we got the satellite phones that morning, the satellite company had changed their programming, so we were doin' all the right numbers but it wasn't working! We're sayin', 'What's goin' on?'"

The phones needed to be upgraded. That was fine for three of them, but the one in Willits couldn't because their Internet service was out. Someone brought it to the top of the grade where they could get Internet, upgraded it, got it to work, and took it back to the hospital. They were back on track. "Now what we do quarterly, we call each other on these phones, 'Hello, is this working?' 'Yes, I hear you fine.' 'Okay, thank you; talk to you in three months.'"

What follows is a series of events and decisions that were made by Sheriff All-man and reported to me. Some were glitches impossible to have foretold at the time. Some are successful decisions that bear retelling. They're not necessarily reported in chronological order.

Law enforcement agencies confer at a barricade in Willits.
Photo by Ree Slocum.

"One thing that really impressed me was that Redwood Valley had an acting fire chief. During the fires last year their fire chief was out for a medical situation, so they had a young acting chief. Well, at first you'd raise your eyebrows and say, 'Oh, my gosh! I need an old salt in there who's seen everything.' But Brandon did a great job. Everything he touched was good. He made a decision that first night that I wouldn't have made, and he made the right decision. Potter Valley had the first fire. They called for Redwood Valley fire engines. Redwood Valley has their fire station and Potter Valley needed it. It was gonna take between twenty and thirty minutes to get to Potter Valley. Brandon had called everyone telling them they'd be going to Potter, but when they got to the Redwood Valley Fire Station and looked up in the hills in the northeast someone said, 'Look at those headlights!' Brandon looked and said, 'Those aren't headlights—that's fire! And we're not going to Potter Valley, we're staying here and heading to the north end of the valley.' It was a brilliant move. Brandon did a stellar job. It was one of those things of using common sense. He knew the winds had shifted and headed west.

"CAL FIRE Chief George Gonzales and I are good friends. We talk at least once a week. When a fire breaks out, he and I are joined at the hip. There's not just the responsibilities, there are legal requirements: the sheriff is constitutionally the one who declares a disaster requiring evacuation; and firefighters, for the most part, are the ones who declare it safe to return. Well, that's not the way it works here. If firefighters come to me and say, 'Hey, we need to evacuate this community because of fire,' I would say, 'I'll order the evacuation on the condition that those residents can return as soon as it's safe.' So George Gonzales and I are good enough friends that I understand his responsibility and he understands mine. I trust him."

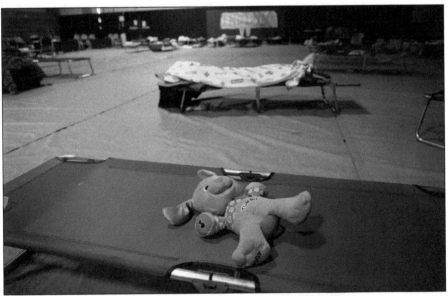

Evacuation Center in Willits. Photo by Ree Slocum.

Sheriff Allman pointed out that when there's a mandatory evacuation notice, the sheriffs and firefighters aren't going to drag landowners from their homes. "We don't take anybody kicking and screaming, because, number one, I'm a property rights kinda guy. If this is your property and you want to stay there and I've given you all the information I have and you still make that decision, all right, knock yourself out! However, if you decide to go we'll do whatever we can to get you a place to go and get you back in as soon as possible when it's safe."

Another change the sheriff instituted was who could declare a Reverse 911. "Certainly we learned from the Emergency Notification too, because we had our Reverse 911 set up so that only lieutenants and above could do the Reverse 911. Well, I don't care if I have a twenty-one-year-old deputy sheriff—if I trust him enough to carry a gun and badge, I trust him enough to call an emergency. So what we did was give every fire chief a card with simple instructions so they and our deputy sheriffs can make a Reverse 911." It worked to help citizens keep abreast of evacuation notices, road closures, bans lifted, and so on, in their immediate areas.

A county sheriff also has a lot of power to get things done and purchase things that are needed to solve current problems. "Carmel Angelo, the CEO, never once told me no for things we needed," said Sheriff Allman. "And the fire departments were doing everything they could, and people said, 'Sheriff, why don't I have phone service in Willits?' That's where I felt most vulnerable. I couldn't help people who were good people. I don't have the power to fix it. I'm sure not going to yell at the phone company and tell them to fix the service. What I say is, 'Tell me what you need me to do.' So we took many phone people up there when nobody else could get up there." He sighed. "And I felt the powerlessness of not getting people back to their homes because of actual fire. Those community talks in Willits, Redwood Valley, and Rec Grove? Let me tell you, I wasn't very popular with some fire departments around the state!"

Cal Fire Conference. Photo by CAL FIRE.

"Radio stations KZYX and KOZT were hugely helpful to us. Two others, KWINE and KUKI, were great—they've never failed me; however, KZYX and KOZT were just 24/7: 'This road is closed, this is what's open, this is when the next community meeting is gonna happen.' And I say, 'Yeah!' because it causes people to say, 'Okay, I can go home and go to sleep.'

"If the lessons of 2017 can be taught to government and nongovernment lead-

Above the Smoke. Painting by Janet Rosen.

ers for the next fifty years, I'd probably say—I can't say it's worth it, because we lost precious lives—but we did the best we could. There were three things that, if we as Mendocino County don't historically remember, we're doomed: 1) We had just come out of a five-year drought; 2) We had Santa Ana winds and NOAA had put out red-flag warnings; and 3) CAL FIRE reporting that we'd gone through forty days where the relative humidity, even at nighttime, was less than 40 percent. During the day it was in the single digits, only 7 to 9 percent. So I certainly want to make sure that the after-action report that's been made will always be in the office of the sheriff, and whoever replaces me, and those down the line, will know these things and be prepared. We must remember this stuff. In 1964 there was a fire very similar to what we saw last year. Well, no one told me that till last year! The old timers said, 'Back in '64 we had somethin' like this!' Really? I didn't know that!"

"I love Mendocino County, not just the fact that we live here and I work here, but I love the people, the environment, I love everything about it. And when you start seeing disasters happen and take away family and friends of people you know, or their property, it really hurts. It's not like you're watching a tsunami in India and you say, 'Oh, that's bad!' and change the channel to sports. You say 'Oh, man! What'll we do?"

"Without getting into the politics of climate change, if anyone on Earth believes that things aren't changing, I'd like to talk to them about that. I don't want to argue whether it's caused by man or by nature or the rotation of the Earth and we're just in a cycle. The first agreement is that things are changing. Fire season in Mendocino County used to be from June 1 to Halloween. We know that we now have wildfires both before June 1 and after Halloween."

The sheriff answered my final question by texts the next day: "Do you have a belief system, a religious or spiritual practice, maybe, that helps you through?"
"While I'm a Christian, my mechanism for dealing with stress involves good friends and great humor. I'm lucky to have a small circle of confidants who listen and advise."

Great advice from a strong leader.

Mendocino Lake Complex Fire:
Escape the Only Option
Written by Carole Brodsky
Originally published in the Ukiah Daily Journal on
October 13, 2017. Used with permission.

Jan Hoyman sits calmly in her studio, placing spouts on ceramic teapots.

The Redwood Valley businesswoman is the owner of the iconic creamery building on Ukiah's Main Street, a place of beauty and serenity, and the site where she has created and sold countless ceramic wares. There are few local residents who don't own a Hoyman mug or an entire dinner set, each hand-painted with flora, fauna, and scenes that evoke the uniqueness of Mendocino County life.

Watching as she expertly works at the potting wheel, it's incomprehensible to imagine that, four days earlier, Hoyman and her neighbors had endured a battle for survival, a struggle that came only a hair's breadth from an unspeakably tragic conclusion.

Hoyman lives off Tomki Road. Though the fire didn't originate in this area, it roared west into the north end of Redwood Valley, where oak trees stud steep ridges, and crisp autumn leaves create inches-deep carpets of duff. The normally dry season, compounded by unseasonably low humidity, set the stage for the conflagration. To date, about one quarter of the total number of individuals who perished in all the fires throughout northern California lived in or around the Tomki Road area.

"I don't even know what time I woke up," says Hoyman, who notes that an antenna that assists with boosting her phone signal wasn't working. "I didn't get any phone calls, but not because my neighbors didn't try."

What woke Hoyman were multiple "Boom, boom, booms" of exploding propane tanks.

"I heard a roar like a locomotive. Then I began to smell smoke. This took maybe a minute. I realized there was a fire, and that it was right here, right on my property."

Still in her nightgown and slippers, Hoyman jumped out of bed and grabbed her dog. "I left my phone and my glasses under my pillow."

She rushed to her Subaru and was trying to coax the dog into the car when she heard her neighbor, Charlotte, honking her horn. "Charlotte was coming down the road from her home, which is higher up than mine. As I got down my road to the main ranch road, there she was. Charlotte's car, with her four children inside, had gone off the road."

Hoyman helped Charlotte load her kids into the Subaru. "I remember saying to Charlotte, 'We're going to get out of here.'"

But as they continued down the driveway toward the ranch road, entire trees were ablaze on both sides of the road. "We weren't even close to the end of my driveway. Thirty-foot trees were burning. We continued driving, and a downed tree, on fire, blocked the driveway. We had no choice but to turn back."

Going about 30 miles an hour, Hoyman backed up her driveway until they reached a gully.

"We decided to drive down the gully and into a nearby vineyard, but when we got there, the vineyard was afire, so we turned around and headed back uphill."

Charlotte implored Hoyman to speed up. "She said, 'Drive faster, drive faster! She offered to drive. Charlotte sped up this wicked-bad road, and somehow my little Subaru made it."

The group made it to Charlotte's house, where her husband, Tom, decided their best option was to take a chainsaw to the burning tree in the driveway below. "By then the fire was so intense he couldn't get close to that tree, so he turned around and met us back at their house."

Tree plate by Jan Hoyman.

The group could see the fire burning below them, and there was no other way out but up. Fortunately, Hoyman discovered she had a pair of shoes and some pants in her car. "We collected water, backpacks, and flashlights. Then we jumped into two four-wheel drive vehicles and headed for Rattlesnake Rock. I couldn't have gotten there myself, even though I'd been there before."

At a certain point, the group had to continue on foot. They headed toward the home of another resident. "We hiked up and down, up and down, to a house on the Willits side of Pine Mountain."

Though that neighbor wasn't home, there was a four-wheeler parked on the property. Miraculously, the keys were still in the ignition.

"Tom found a trailer and attached it to the four-wheeler. There were seven of us plus my dog. We went about a mile up the road when the trailer got a flat tire. We tried to decide what to do, thinking maybe we should split up, with one of us taking the kids and continuing to walk, but we decide to stick together."

Then the next miracle occurred: "We ran into a couple of young guys who lived nearby. One of them, Norman, has a beater truck—yay! Beater trucks don't melt," Hoyman smiles.

Norman packed the group into his truck. "It was freezing. None of us had jackets, and by then it was freezing cold. We passed two checkpoints, and no one could tell us if the roads were open ahead of us, but people told us to go and go now. By then I was so disoriented I couldn't tell where we were, but apparently we were near Baker Creek Road."

Norman took the group all the way to the Willits Police Department, which took at least another half hour. "He was such a nice man. By then, it was about 4 a.m. There were great, great people at the PD. We got checked in and were given blankets and water, food and donuts. Everyone was great to my dog, who was being overly friendly," Hoyman smiles.

"I believe it was Lisa Epstein of the Willits Chamber of Commerce who kept us posted as information started to trickle in. Everyone was incredible—so thoughtful, making sure we were comfortable."

Once TV service was established, all the coverage was focused on the Sonoma County fires. "There was no cell service, and I didn't have a phone anyway. One person passed her phone around to anyone who needed it. The adrenaline began to wear off, and I realized I needed to contact my kids."

Hoyman's son lived near Piner Road in Santa Rosa, and was also in the midst of evacuating. "He was okay and I was okay."

Other neighbors from the Frey Ranch and Rancho Mariposa began arriving at the police station. "We began checking in and felt like most of our people were accounted for. At that point we decided to get back to Ukiah via Fort Bragg."

Hoyman traveled with her neighbor, Cathy Monroe, and Tom returned home, where he was able to save the family home and Hoyman's car. "Tom put water on his house and my car until all the plastic water pipes melted."

As soon as they arrived in Fort Bragg, Monroe and Hoyman stopped at Harvest Market. "After all, that's where you go when you get to Fort Bragg. We got out to get something to drink, and there's our whole group, recongregated. We shared more stories, drove through Boonville, and headed to Ukiah, where I've been ever since."

Hoyman has a place to stay with a friend for as long as necessary. "My bookkeeper came to work and asked what I needed. I didn't have a car, and she offered an extra vehicle for me."

Fire plate by Jan Hoyman.

Jan Hoyman has lived in Ukiah for over forty years, and is known not only for her pottery but for her commitment to her community, supporting her employees with a real living wage, helping local nonprofit organizations, and creating a sustainable business model that has thrived through decades of social and economic fluctuation. Now, the community she loves is giving back to her.

"The outpouring of gracious neighborliness is overwhelming. We live in a community that is together, a community that truly strives to be there for each other. It doesn't matter that we lost our homes. That will matter later. Right now, we have a great community to live in."

Though Hoyman has not been allowed back to her home, she is fairly certain it was completely destroyed. She is cautiously optimistic that Norman and his friend made it out safely. "The Search and Rescue team asked Tom to take them up the ridge, the same way we'd hiked, to see if Norman and his friend were safe. Both of their vehicles were gone, but the team continued searching the area to see if there were others who might not have made it."

When Hoyman was finally able to speak with her son following his evacuation, he said something that truly touched her: "Mom, you live in the right place, because you have community. But guess what? Now I know my neighbors too."

Hoyman still has a business to run and inventory to build as the holiday season draws near. But her priorities are clear.

"I'm so glad I'm still alive."

Ada's Story
Written by Carole Brodsky

"The gophers survived!" Redwood Valley resident Ada B. Fine called out to her life partner Doug Smith. When the couple returned to their home for the first time, it was about ten days after their evacuation from the Mendocino Lake Complex Fire, which tore through their neighborhood and changed their lives forever.

In their former backyard, the presence of a freshly dug gopher hole signified so much—survival and rebirth, as opposed to pesky varmints wreaking havoc in their garden, which was no more.

The couple had lived in their home for eleven years, the longest either had lived in one place, including their childhood homes. Both are multi-decade residents of Mendocino County. Ada is well known in the arts, education, and therapeutic communities as a gifted multimedia artist and instructor. Currently she is an Art Specialist at Tapestry Family Services. She works part-time making art with Tapestry clients, children ranging from ages seven to twelve. Ada has taught art to children and adults since 1981 as a private instructor at the Mendocino Art Center, Mendocino College, and at local schools as a recipient of several grants, including one from the California Arts and Schools program.

Following the fire, her studio and her home became one of hundreds of toxic rubble piles—what insurance companies deemed a "total loss."

Part refuge, part mini-classroom for her students, Ada's studio was her sanctuary. Her collage materials were neatly labeled and arranged according to content. Shallow vintage boxes holding cutouts, magazine pages, greeting cards, advertisements, and every possible kind of ephemera were carefully catalogued, destined to become part of an art piece—usually a combination of drawing, painting, and collage, or an item that would be shared with her students when they needed a particular image for a project.

The living room was Doug's place to relax. A retired mechanic, Doug is approaching his sixty-sixth birthday, and this one was to be a real celebration, as he had recently survived a bout with cancer and has been dealing with several significant ailments for many years. Along with cars, Doug's passion is music, and one wall of their living room was filled top to bottom with his vinyl and CD collection. "I had one record by King Crimson. I think that album was worth quite a bit of money," he muses. But it wasn't the monetary value of his collection that broke Doug's heart; it was the loss of his music, which represented a significant part of his daily life and routine.

A station wagon, trucks, and a motorcycle of Doug's were damaged beyond repair, and his entire collection of tools was destroyed. "My Estwing hammer was destroyed. It sounds silly, but wow, I loved that hammer."

Ada was working in her studio at 1:15 a.m. on the night the fire broke out. She noticed the smell of smoke, and at that moment Doug entered her studio saying they'd gotten a call from a friend in Potter Valley suggesting they evacuate. "Right about then, one of our neighbors came to the door and said we should leave immediately," said Ada.

"When I looked outside, it was like a fire tornado. It was hitting the hills and swirling and twirling. I didn't look for long, because I knew we had to get the heck out of there," said Doug. "I'd never been in a firestorm like that."

"We got out within ten minutes," said Ada. "I looked out our front door, and it looked to me like the fire was across the street. We could see flames, which is why we left so quickly. We knew that if we could see the fire, it could be too late for us, so we got out."

The couple left without their chickens, ducks, and the two feral cats they'd cared for since they were kittens.

"We were able to grab some clothes and I grabbed some of my handmade jewelry," Ada noted. "I half expected we'd be able to come back. I didn't want to go too far away because we wanted to return and check on our animals. We didn't realize at that point how close the fire was to our house."

They decided to drive toward the Mendocino Coast. "I knew most of our friends would have to work first thing in the morning, so we didn't want to bother anyone," Ada said. They pulled onto the side of the road and decided to sleep for a few hours. The pair did not have cell phones, so friends were unable to reach them, and they had no way to receive up-to-date information about the spread of the fire.

"We came back to West Road Monday morning and found out that our house had quite likely burned down. We decided the best thing to do was stay on the coast where the air was cleaner," Ada continued. Both Doug and Ada had lived on the coast for a period of time. "We were well taken care of by our circle of friends on the coast who we've known and loved for years," said Ada.

Ada still mourns what were once tens of thousands of pages of books and magazines. At their homesite following the fire, the slightest breeze turned the pure-white pages into nothing but tiny ash, as they became, literally, "gone with the wind." Ada had a significant collection—hundreds of art books and children's books, which she used in her teaching to provide inspiration, to learn about specific artists, or to develop new ideas. Over the decades she amassed a vast collection of paints, every type and size of drawing, painting, and watercolor paper, scissors, stickers, glue, glitter, pencils, pastels, T-squares and rulers, paper-making supplies, and every kind of collage imagery imaginable.

Perhaps the most poignant part of their property tour came with the realization that Ada's most deeply personal art work had been completely destroyed: a papier mâché chihuahua, a multimedia series she made following the death of her mother, Valentine's Day cards she had made for Doug, and many more works of art made by Ada and other artists. "The only saving grace is that I'd gotten a large portion of my art photographed over the years, and I'd had enough presence of mind to grab those slides on the way out," she said.

"The couple started completely over again. They were renters, and as for so many fire survivors, no amount of insurance could cover personal items that were by definition entirely irreplaceable. "We were so lucky to have a friend with a spare bedroom. John was gracious enough to accommodate us for several weeks following the fire," said Ada."

"People were so generous," Doug said. While on the coast, they were able to assemble a new wardrobe—shopping at thrift stores and accepting clothing donated by friends. "When I first came to Mendocino County as a single guy about thirty-five years ago, I had a sleeping bag, clothes, a motorcycle, and tools. Immediately following the fires, I had less than that. But guess what? While I was rummaging through a satchel, I found my Pierre Cardin robe and my Teva sandals. It's the little things. Finding these two items was like finding old friends," said Doug, grinning from ear to ear.

Doug's robe was especially precious because it had belonged to Ada's father, who passed away many years ago. The sandals made it easier for Doug to enjoy his annual birthday soak at Orr Hot Springs, a years-old tradition they were determined to continue.

"All my paperwork that I'd never tended to— many years, many piles—it all burned up! We left with our wits, and even today all we have left is our wit," Ada laughs.

And perhaps the best news of all? "The cats made it," said Ada. She recalls returning to her homesite to meet with FEMA reps. "It was raining, and Peachy, one of our feral cats, was crouched in Doug's burned-out truck. It was so dark, so sad, and so depressing, but life continued."

The couple had no plans to move the feral cats to a new location, and neighbors committed to look out for the cats, assuring that they were well cared for during the weeks following the blaze.

Sharing a bedroom at their friend's home, Ada and Doug began the years-long process of rebuilding their lives.

"The best part of living at John's house was being in a stable, clean household that was rhythmic and set up. For a time, I didn't have to think about looking for another house. For two and a half months, John's home was a comfortable, warm, safe bubble, and we really needed that. I'm so thankful he was able to put us up," Ada said.

Ada and Doug were able to find permanent housing in January 2018. "The place we're currently renting fell into our lap. We avoided moving to this new home for a bit. For me, moving meant never going back to our place in Redwood Valley. It was permanent. I'd been avoiding those feelings for some time," Ada said.

"For me, in the paradigm of 'flight, fright, or freeze,' I was frozen for months and months after the fires, even though our community, our friends, and loved ones came together, donating money, furniture, and art supplies. I would just stare at the walls. I'd sit and look at the swirls of paint—that was enough stimulus for me. Even with all the support we've received, it's been really hard, but the kindness of the community has helped us cope. People I don't even know donated to our recovery fund," Ada said.

To make matters more complex, Ada has a health condition. In April 2018, she required back-to-back surgeries, from which she has now recovered.

It's been difficult for Ada and Doug to adjust to "living in town."

"I miss the rural setting. Even though all my art, my books, and heirlooms are gone, what I miss most is the sound of the frogs, the opossums that came up on the back porch, and our duck pond. I miss the sound of birds, the trees, and the views. I miss the landscape. But I don't miss the raccoons," she laughed. "Living in town is a whole new way of life. But it's what we needed for our physical health."

Ada became a participant in an "Art From the Ashes" workshop, and created an individual mosaic for a community art show. "I would sit beside other women, creating artwork with remnants of my life that made it through the fire." Ada made a piece entitled What I Miss the Most, which featured duck, songbird, and chicken imagery, enhanced by a blackened heart-shaped tin that she embellished with beads melted by the fire.

"We didn't have much that made it," Ada explained. "As I was working on this piece, I think I realized for the first time how much I don't have: the antique paper scraps, vintage images of chickens, my beads, even practical items like the many types of glue I collected and used for various projects. This doesn't make me sad as much as it makes me frustrated."

Ada and Doug's Redwood Valley home was one of Ada's favorite places to live. "I can still see Doug, watching him tend the property, and feed the chickens and the ducks. There was a beautiful rhythm to our days, and we haven't acclimated to the in-town rhythm yet," she explained.

Creating a functional art studio space has proven challenging. "We have a really nice space, which is also significantly smaller than the home we lost. I now have a desk and a bookcase instead of a separate studio." Ada's dream is to find a way to recreate a studio where she can continue to make art for herself and teach students. The feelings of "overwhelm" continue, particularly as Ada returned to work following her surgeries. There's an arts grant she needs to apply for. She needs to regain momentum at work, attend physical therapy sessions, do her daily exercise program, and complete the process of evaluating her business losses. "I'm finding it hard not to feel completely inundated. I feel incapable of moving forward at times, to just put one foot in front of the other."

Being out in public has been challenging, particularly for Ada. "It's difficult to retell our story again and again, even though I know people ask because they care about us and want to know how I'm doing. I'm often not sure what to say. Sometimes I just quack," she laughs. "So far, the Mendocino Book Company and the library are the places I feel safest. Attending events has been very challenging for me. Maybe being in our sixties and starting all over again has been part of what's been so hard for us. It's been both interesting and difficult at the same time."

Recently Ada and Doug drove by their former home. "We've been here only a few times since the fire. I'm still shocked by the absence of what was there. It's all been graded over.

"This is still my home, and our desire is to stay here in Mendocino County. We're still going one day at a time, because there's still so much I have to do to get my life in order. When I think about something I want for the long term—how to reestablish my life for today and for the future—it still seems so nebulous and intangible to me, more than a year after the fires changed our lives," she concluded.

Mike Doody and his partner, Ziggy Daniels, survey the remains of their home on West Road. Photo by Mike Doody.

Fire Self-Defense:
Michael Trevey's Story
Written by Ree Slocum

"Fire Self-Defense: A local's story about protecting his property during last month's Redwood fire," by Ree Slocum, was originally published in the November 2, 2017 edition of Willits Weekly, www.willitsweekly.com. At the time, Michael Trevey didn't want his last name in the article; thus he is known as "Michael" in this reprint of the original. Photos from the article are not included.

Following Michael's harrowing story is Mary Ann's own heart-wrenching account in "Mary Anne Trevey's Story: The Other Side of the Trevey Couple's Fire Experience," written by Ree Slocum from an interview on August 8, 2018, ten months after the Mendocino Complex Fire.

Michael and Mary Anne have been living on their remote, densely wooded, and steep-sided canyon property on the Redwood Valley side of Pine Mountain subdivision for over forty years. When they started to homestead, they had only a few water tanks with pipes running on the ground to a variety of destinations. The couple realized the family's vulnerability to wildfires, and their water needs also increased as they added gardens, fruit trees, and animals. Through the years Michael has made tremendous improvements to the original simple water system.

"Right now we have 20,000 to 30,000 gallons stored in poly tanks and gravity fed in buried lines to our home, shop, and gardens. We have two pools in our year-round creek, one near the house and the other near the shop. There's a water pump by each," he said, and added, "Last year I put in three fire hydrants, each with a 200-foot hose." There's an impressive 110 pounds of pressure through those hoses. These recent additions were essential in saving his property during the raging fire a few weeks ago.

At about 1:30 in the morning of Monday, October 9, Michael and Mary Anne were awakened by Mary Anne's ringing phone as well as their renter's pounding on the door to alert them to the fires. Michael went to the top of his driveway, and it was "a crimson sky with a hurricane sound, you know. I went up there, looked over the side, saw the flames coming up through the trees, and I said, 'Oh, geez, we gotta get outta here!' I came down and loaded up Mary Anne and the dogs, and took my truck up to a neighbor's place, then came back to get the other truck.

"In the meantime Mary Anne had left. I put my excavator in the creek so it wouldn't burn. I was moving my backhoe so it wouldn't burn, when I realized that the fire hadn't come whooping over the hill and roaring down here like a crown or canopy fire. You can't fight those. You have to leave."

What he noticed next was little fires on his hillsides around him that were creeping down toward the house, gardens, storage barn, and chicken coop. He said to himself, "Well, I've got defensible space. I've got the water. I've got the hoses. And it isn't a crown fire!" So he decided to stay and battle the encroaching flames.

By 6 a.m. when Michael called Mike Dawson, a ranch hand, to come and help him fight the fires, Michael had the hoses hooked up to the hydrants. He'd been wetting down the cleared hillsides around his house, and wetting the house and the rest of the clearing and buildings. He used the hose in the garden to wet the hillside and fenceposts. He'd also hopped on the quad, checking the roads and wetting the surrounding area around his workshop a quarter mile away.

Dawson made it through before the checkpoints closed the roads. "No Mikey. No ranch!" Michael emailed. The next forty-eight hours were a constant vigil with no sleep for Michael. The wind whipped up, showering embers in every direction and starting fires. At one point during the worst of the fire, flames began climbing up the tall redwoods not twenty feet from his wood-sided home. Thankfully they'd been limbed up seventy feet, and Michael was able to quell the fire using water from the fire hydrant and hose he'd so recently installed.

Putting out small and larger fires that crept to the edges of his clearings and garden fence, and keeping the road open that runs from Pine Mountain to West Road in Redwood Valley, were priorities. The back road was the emergency road that firefighters used as well as evacuees. Michael and Dawson used the backhoe and excavator to move the fallen trees off of the road. Michael's land partner, Scott, stayed a few crucial days, monitoring the fire on the Internet and riding his quad on the roads, reporting back to Michael about trees that were down and giving him updates about the fire.

By Wednesday, air support started coming in, dropping water and retardant. Tanker trucks and crews from different states came into Pine Mountain to create firebreaks. By evening most of the crisis was over for Michael and Dawson. The winds had died down. The hundred-foot clearing uphill from the house held, as did most of the rest of the cleared space. Fire had just licked at the majority of the garden fence. The house, shop, chicken coop, and chickens, along with the storage barn, were saved. Michael could finally sleep.

The redwood mother stump in the little redwood grove next to the couple's house was still burning deep in the ground at the time of our interview, twenty days after the fire. Mary Anne recalled seeing embers float up into the air as she looked out the living-room window one night after she returned home. Her husband didn't believe her at first, probably because he'd soaked the stump with water. He went out and soaked it again, and yet again when we were there talking and saw a wisp of smoke trailing up the side of the newly charred redwood. Evidently there are "smokers" like that created by fires. The fire goes deep into the ground, following the stumps or trunks of trees down through their root systems. They can burn a long time. Firefighters are still dealing with some of these.

The losses on Michael and Mary Anne's property were minimal. "Two of my water tanks burned. Each was separate to the water system, and some aboveground poly pipe that I'd put off burying burned like a fuse. Oh, and the burn pile is now gone!"

Michael doesn't begin to consider himself a hero. "I've got three essential things going on here," he explained: "30,000 gallons of stored water with buried pipes and 110 pounds of pressure; maybe another 20,000 gallons in the creek with the pumps close by, and situational awareness"—the ability to see what's going on and what it means in the big picture.

"Don't let a barn fire distract you from a canopy fire roaring in that closes off exit routes and makes you a dead fool," he emailed me later as an explanation. "I had time. The people in Redwood Valley didn't!" he said Sunday as he looked in the distance with moist eyes. "And we lucked out, because the fire was burning downhill, which was slower and gave us time."

Michael sends a big thank-you, again, to the Nevada County, Santa Clara County, Novato, and Smith River Hotshots crews and all our local crews. They saved the top parcel cabin by an inch!

Since the worst fires in Mendocino County history have hit us, it isn't a wonder that people have renewed and urgent concerns about what they can do to be fire safe.

Not everyone lives like Michael and Mary Anne, or has the sensibility, infrastructure, or skills to defend their home. CAL FIRE has pamphlets and other publications like a "Homeowners Checklist: How to make your home fire safe," to name just one handy and thorough booklet. They may have enough staff and available time for someone to come out and check your defensible space to see if you meet

Photo by Ree Slocum.

regulations, and to give you needed information.

If your home or property isn't defensible, CAL FIRE won't put their firefighters at risk of injury or death. You can visit their website at www.calfire.ca.gov or go to www. readyforwildfire.org for further information on home and property safety measures.

Photo by Ree Slocum.

Mary Anne Trevey's Story:
The Other Side of the Treveys' Fire Experience
Written by Ree Slocum

Mary Anne remembers a text coming through early Monday, October 9, from her friend and neighbor Elaine. What Elaine texted about the little-known fire was, "Look out your back door…it's coming your way and you have to evacuate!" Believing there was little chance the house would survive, Mary Anne and Michael got the car loaded with important things: the family photo albums, money, their passports, some winter clothes, the three dogs, and dog food. They had plenty of time, since the fire was still over the mountain in Redwood Valley—they lived a few miles up a steep canyon just north and west of the Frey Ranch.

When Michael and Mary Anne left in separate vehicles, both believed they were evacuating to Marta and Chris Bartow, their daughter and son-in-law's home outside Willits. When they got to the top of their property, Mary Anne proceeded along the still-clear road to Willits. She knew Michael had decided there was time to head back down to the property and move the excavator and backhoe to the creek bottom where they might survive the fire; but it was also the time when Michael noticed that it wasn't a crown fire. Knowing he had everything in place to defend the property, he decided to stay.

Mary Anne got to Marta and Chris' home. "I remember getting to my daughter's and sobbing, 'I think we're going to lose everything! It's coming, and I don't see how we can prevent it from destroying our property!'" They made her some tea and she went to sleep on their couch, still unaware that Michael had decided to stay on the property and defend it.

When Mary Anne woke up later that day, most of the power in Willits was shut off, and there was no cell service—the Treveys had no service on their property anyway. "That was the beginning of three days of total hell! My husband never did show up. I had no idea if he was still down there or not. I had no idea if my house was still there. There were no communications at all," she told me. "So I went through a couple of days feeling sick and unable to eat anything, just being really upset." Mary Anne is the owner of Mariposa Market in Willits. During her three hellish days of not knowing whether Michael was still alive or if her home had survived the fire, she worked. "The first few days were really super-hard," she remembered. "There were employees from Redwood Valley who couldn't make it to work. I really had to be there." She found the distraction was good for her. It kept some of the uncertainty at bay because she had to be fully at work.

Then Wednesday rolled around. Mary Anne woke up crying, and said to her son-in-law, "Chris you've gotta find out what happened!"

Chris said, "I'm going to get up there one way or the other."

At that point Pine Mountain was blockaded, a mandatory evacuation notice in place. "Somehow he finagled his way into getting up there. I don't know how he did it!" Mary Anne laughed, reliving her relief. "When he got to the top of our property there were people who knew that Michael was still alive and had actually saved our house, and that was all I heard. I didn't know about the outbuildings or the barn. It was seven more days before I saw Michael again or got home!" At some point she'd accepted the fact that they might have lost everything and would have to start over. "That was the part I didn't want to think about," she admitted.

After ten days of more unknowns, the mandatory evacuation ban was lifted and the couple reunited at home. "It was exciting to see Michael; he'd done all this stuff, you know. By then we were coming down from the whole situation, and of course I was really glad to see him, but he was distracted and talked, talked, talked about what had happened and what he'd done. He was still wound up!"

Even though Mary Anne was happy to be home she was far from feeling safe. "Hotspots were burning everywhere! There were two big ones right behind the house, and I was really nervous and didn't sleep well." There were stumps still on fire deep in the ground—she would see the sparks at night. "It was scary because all it would take was a wind and the sparks could start another fire. And it was still warm and dry." After CDF came down and put out all the hotspots with water and retardant, the couple felt relief from the fear of renewed fire on their property. A week or so later it rained and the fire season was over. The Treveys, along with everyone else in the county, breathed fresh air!

When I asked Mary Anne what helped her through those freaky times when she wasn't working she said, "There were several people staying at my daughter's house. We'd all been evacuated, so we did a lot of talking and we tried to eat dinner together. It felt like there was a lot of support, and that got me through. A couple of those first nights I dreamt that they found Michael, just a skeleton, hanging onto the four-wheeler, which was all burned up. It was a horrifying dream—it was during those first three nights—it was horrifying and no one knew what happened to him." As I was leaving her office at the market, Mary Anne added, "And I prayed... a lot!"

Tara's Story
Written by Ree Slocum

Tara Manolian, her husband, Johnny, and their son, Harry, moved to Redwood Valley from Humboldt County in June 2017, four months before the Mendocino Complex Fire. Harry turned five the week before the fire. The couple moved to the Frey Ranch in order to work and learn biodynamic farming with Luke Frey. "It was our new start, our new beginning," Tara told me, with a catch in her voice. "We were so excited! It was a dream come true, something we always wanted to learn about and practice, so we moved. We loved the house. My dad came out from Colorado to stay for a week and help us make improvements to it. We were fixing our decks and putting in new light fixtures. This was going to be our long-term house. Harry had started pre-K at the Buddhist School in Talmage, and ahh, life was good. We were as happy as we've ever been."

Tara is a soft-spoken, petite woman in her mid-thirties. Her voice broke often as she described—almost step by step—her escape with Harry and their dog, Chiefy, from the fiery inferno that sped toward her and threatened their lives that night. She revealed that she's been to "talk therapy" and learned to go to her "safe place" when emotions get overwhelming. There were many pauses in our interview as she composed herself and continued telling her harrowing experiences evacuating Redwood Valley on that fateful night when she and the family lost all of their earthly possessions.

Sunday nights Tara ironed Harry's uniforms for school for the week, sometimes staying up late. The Sunday night of the fire, she stayed up until eleven in order to clean house for the busy week ahead. At 1 a.m. Tara was woken from a "deep sleep" by the ding of a text coming in on the computer in the next room. "For some reason it woke me, and it was Johnny. He was staying at the Foot Hills, not staying with us that night. He was down the street. The text had no sense of urgency whatsoever. It just said, 'Are you up?' I responded, 'Well, I am now!' I didn't smell smoke, but I got up and looked out the window. I noticed an orange glow, but it was in the west, not where it was supposed to be as far as sunrise goes. I texted Johnny back and said, 'What's that glow?' I thought maybe he'd awakened me to see the aurora borealis or something, but as soon as I texted, 'What's that glow?' it occurred to me, and I texted, 'Fire?'"

"Johnny didn't text me back, so I went outside, and sure enough I could hear my neighbors, who were in their twenties, whooping it up: 'Woohoo, fiiire!' I thought, this is very strange, and all at once it hit me. As it did, a huge gust of wind came, and I will never forget that sound!"

Tara broke down and paused for a while as she gathered the determination and strength to continue through her tears. "I could hear it and see it, and there was just this wall. And it jumped in that moment, in that gust, it jumped... like so far I couldn't believe it! It was just coming at me so fast!"

Tara took a few more moments to come back from those terrifying images in her memory and into the safety of our little room at the Ukiah Library. "It was so powerful and loud. I knew then what was happening, so I ran back inside, and at that point a FaceTime call was coming in—the Internet was still working. It was Johnny. He was at the intersection of Tomki and West Roads. Then I saw emergency lights flashing in the background. He told me, 'They're stopping me here. I can't get back to you. You can't come this way. You have to go back! You have to go through the forest, through the woods. I want you out now! It's coming that way!' and then we got cut off. I don't remember exactly how we left it."

At that point Tara tried to get her pants on under her pajamas. Harry was still in his bed asleep. She ran into his room and got pants for him. "I woke up Harry, and it took everything I had to stay calm and not scare him. I told him, 'Harry, there's a fire, and it's dangerous and we have to go right now.' He didn't know what I was talking about. I picked him up and grabbed his pants and we just went straight out to the car. I didn't think of taking anything else. I put a pair of shoes on, and put Harry in his seat. I could just hear that roar!"

Once again Tara took time to calm. "The dog had followed me out. We have a Mastiff. He's a big dog, and he's afraid of the car, so as soon as Harry was in his seat I just picked up the dog and stuffed him in the seat next to Harry. Storm, our cat, had been there next to me too, so I picked him up and tried to get him into the car, but he tore my arm up and jumped right out of my arms! I said, 'We have to go!' and Harry was upset that Storm was left. I pulled out of the driveway and slowly and carefully made my way out of there. You know I didn't see anybody walking around. I didn't see the kids next door…anything. I didn't see any of the Freys till I got to Tomki. Oh, but I knew to head north into the woods 'cause of what Johnny had told me, so I made that left, and when I was passing the winery I remember seeing, I think it was John Frey and Katrina. They were at the end of their road about to turn onto Tomki too. I'll never forget this detail: a plastic bag had blown out of their car, and John, bless his heart, not wanting to litter, he goes after that plastic bag!" she laughed, "Yeah the things I remember! It gave me a chance to stop, and I said, 'Which way are you going?' He said, 'Going to the forest.' So that's what I did. I'm pretty sure they must've pulled out behind me."

They were all taking the route north up Tomki Road, the back way to Willits known for its gravelly ruggedness and many creek crossings. This was October, so at least there wasn't any water in the creek beds.

"There were cars just flying on that road! A whole line of cars. It was chaos, and I pulled into somebody's driveway and it overlooked the whole thing. I stopped and just watched for a second and tried to make sense of it: 'What the heck is happening?!' You know? And it was close, and, well, I took a picture, not a very good one, but it gives me a timeline to look back on. That was about 1:30. I had twenty minutes... twenty minutes...all that manzanita and everything was between me and the fire," she said, looking far away with a little laugh and then a big sigh.

Tara was driving a minivan and knew she had some stream crossings to navigate on the journey ahead. She saw the rest of the Freys before the first crossing. She stopped to talk with Daniel Frey, Luke and Emily Frey's son, and Daniel gave her some advice about driving the minivan across the streambeds. "He told me, 'Now Tara, stop to think about where your oil pan is, okay?' Good advice, but I didn't know what I was up against. As soon as he said that, I figured out that it was something my car wasn't gonna be able to do, so I parked and I waited because I was terrified. I didn't know what to do, so I just parked on the side of the road and wanted to get more information from Daniel, but cars were flying by my car, and I was so afraid to be on the dark road on foot and get hit. I didn't want to leave Harry and Chiefy in the van and risk them getting hit 'cause people were fishtailing. I mean it was so scary!" Tara felt safe because "I could see the stars. There was no fire where we were." She sat there for quite a while holding Harry on her lap. They talked and watched the

The view of Tara's backyard to the hills that were all burning during their escape. Photo by Tara Manolian.

cars go whizzing by until about 3 a.m. Suddenly, there was Johnny in his truck! He'd gone all the way around from Redwood Valley onto Highway 101 to Willits before the highway closure, then onto the Tomki Road to where Tara was parked on the roadside.

"He was full of adrenaline, of course, and he said, 'Come on! We're doin' this—follow me!' No, let's back up: First of all he said, 'Did you grab anything?'" Tara choked up with tears of regret as she continued with Johnny's questions: "'Did you grab the money?' Our life savings were in a suitcase in the closet. I said, 'No I didn't, and Johnny said, 'Well, I'm gonna go back and try to get it.' Before I could respond he sped off. Then, about fifteen minutes later, he showed back up and said he couldn't get it. It was too late," she said, her voice sad and resigned. "It's a tough one for me, the guilt. And I also know in my heart that I couldn't go back. I couldn't run back in that house. I couldn't leave Harry in the car by himself. He would've been scared and I just knew I had to go, you know? I saw the wall [of fire] and how fast it was going to travel on me and it was fast! Because of the wind it was a hundred yards farther. It was unbelievable!"

When Johnny got back he told Tara to follow him. He reassured her that there were stream crossings, but to just follow him and go the way he went, and they'd be fine.

"So we got to the first stream crossing, but I haven't looked down to see what it looks like. We're right there, and we see a white car. Johnny stops first, and I realize on the right side of this car are fifteen monks just standing around what I think is a Prius."

There was also a woman with them who had a very peaceful presence, and she ended up sitting next to Tara in the passenger seat. There were four monks who were going to get in the back seat with Harry and Chief. "They saw Chiefy and said, 'I think we'll go in the rear,' she told me with a little laugh. "So there were four monks in the rear of the van, and that's another thing I think of: If I had grabbed anything, I wouldn't have had as much room for those people. So that was another big 'I know it happened right' moment. We were all loaded up and I remember two monks in the back of Johnny's truck going for this wild ride and holding on. Oh, my God, I was sure someone was going to get hurt. I was so scared!"

"We got to the next stream crossing. Johnny goes through, and I pull up, and it looked like a fifteen-foot drop."

Tara was sure she was going to drop right off the edge and smash into the creek bottom. She began to cry as she remembered: "I looked back at Harry, and everybody was looking at me with hope in their eyes, you know? Even though I was going to crash right into it, I had to try! I wanted to try for everybody. So we did [she slides her hands together to indicate smoothness]...right through, one after the other, right through!"

The two vehicles full of people made their way safely through the streambeds to

The remains of Tara's treasured camera, from her life as a photographer before the fire. Photo by Tara Manolian.

Willits, where they gathered at the Mariposa Market parking lot. The monks were reunited "and it was, ahh [big sigh], such a relief!"

At that point it was early, and communications were still out of order. Johnny told the group that there were also fires in Santa Rosa. He'd started to think maybe it was a terrorist attack. They were all trying to make sense of what had just happened. It was about 5 or 6 a.m. when a policeman showed up and suggested they go to the emergency shelter at the County Building. When they arrived, Tara remembers, "All my neighbors were there, all the Freys. Gosh, there were elderly people in their bathrobes, and thank goodness people were starting to gather. Around 6:30 we were able to turn the TV on and see what the hell was going on!"
There they learned about the current extent of the two wildfires.

The little family, with Harry and Tara still in their pajamas, went on to Fort Bragg that morning. "We took Harry to the toy store and just let him play at the train. Those two ladies at the toy store took me behind their desk and just let me cry, and gave me water and gave me clothes to wear," her voice breaks. "I didn't know them, you know? Everybody in Fort Bragg was either running from Santa Rosa or from our direction, so we were all kind of in it together. It's amazing! I've never been a part of anything like this…it gives me hope for humanity."

Tara has a long list of people who helped them during their escape from the fire to their current lives in Ukiah. Her thankfulness is on the surface: "So many random acts of kindness!"

Regrets seem to be a part of many people's stories. Tara felt guilty about not yelling to the kids next door as she was leaving. They all made it out safely, but she still felt guilty about being so focused on leaving that she didn't have time to consider much else. It seems she's made peace with leaving the family's life savings behind. She's found treasures in her connections with family, friends, and human kindnesses in her life.

When I asked Tara how Harry has done with losing his home and toys, she perked up and said, "He did great. He was so brave. He never really cried. He never went to sleep. He was just aware. I think he liked getting the new toys. Kids live in the moment. Sometimes he'll say, 'We used to have that,' or 'I used to have that but it all got burned up!' He's just kind of matter-of-fact about it, but the kindness and love that came after has, I think, been more important to him than the loss."

Then it was Tara's turn to tell me if there was anything she's taken away from this experience. "My first takeaway in the weeks after was just that 'things' don't matter at all. When you're stripped of everything it really is a different feeling, but I have such a great family and great friends. Even when I didn't have anything, I had everything!" she sobbed. "I knew it was gonna be okay. Life is more about the connections we make than about the stuff we buy or the awards we get or the clothes we wear…it's about connecting with each other."

I was struck with the realization that this woman before me had had to make some of the quickest and most important decisions of her life. She'd put aside her own terror to forge ahead, seeking the best path to safety for her son and herself. I couldn't help exclaiming, "My God, Tara! You were Superwoman!" She replied, "I had to be. That could've been it, you know?"

I saw Tara a few weeks after our original interview. She said she'd forgotten to add, "The cat lived!"

After three days the couple was let back in to check on things where their house

One of Harry's LEGO pieces. Photo by Tara Manolian.

Top: Tara's home before. **Middle:** after the fire. **Bottom:** after the remnants were scraped and hauled away. Photo by Tara Manolian.

had been. On the road they saw one of the Frey's farm helpers who told them he had their cat. "Sure enough, John went there the next day. Storm's paws were badly burned, and two toes were melted together, but he was alive!"

They took him to Bliss, a veterinarian at the Ukiah Fair Grounds who donated her time to rescued animals. Her adult daughter, Sarah, helped. Bliss wrapped the cat's paws and gave him IV fluids. Firestorm, formerly known as Storm, is now fully recovered due to the veterinarian's care, and miraculously, all the cats at the ranch had shown up in a surviving house at the back of the ranch.

Stormy the cat. Photo by Tara Manolian.

Rudy's Story
Written by Carole Brodsky

Rudy Raya lives alone at the end of a well-maintained gravel road about two miles west of Redwood Valley's West Road. Rudy has lived in his home for two years. An employee at the Mendocino County Department of Transportation, he is purchasing his home from his adoptive parents, Clint and Jane Kelly, longtime Redwood Valley residents and educators. The beautiful rustic home is replete with forty-foot ceilings, a garden bursting with late-season raspberries and tomatoes, and an incredible, copious spring that enabled the Kellys to plant and tend a bountiful orchard of olive trees, figs, apples, and stone fruits. Several garden sheds and small outbuildings provide storage for tools and supplies. A rural home requisite— a large propane tank—is located just a few feet from the main house.

Living high above the valley, Rudy has an exquisite, unobstructed view that encompasses the eastern hills that separate Redwood Valley from Potter Valley. It is a calm, bucolic setting; a model of off-grid living; a rural hideaway that one could imagine on the cover of Sunset magazine.

Rudy's few neighbors also live on large parcels. Over the years, they've looked out for each other and shared tasks, including the upkeep of their rural road, but as Rudy scans his forty-acre property more than a year after the fires, the damage is still terrifyingly evident. The nearby hills, less than 500 yards to the north, were once a wild, majestic oak and pine woodland. Now all that remains are denuded hillocks and blackened skeletons of thousands of trees, clearly visible from Rudy's garden, where the Kellys' cat makes herself comfortable, sunning herself on Clint's garden bench.

A closer examination reveals just how close the fire came to Rudy's home. The solar array, still standing in a south-facing field, is propped up by a two-by-four redwood framework, but upon inspection, one notices that every piece of lumber is charred and profoundly weakened by fire.

"Look at the fenceposts," Rudy says. What few posts remain around the substantial garden and orchard no longer support any fence. They're merely charcoal reminders of what occurred. And what occurred was a night of such terror it's a wonder that even one year after the fire Rudy can muster the courage to tell his story, which by any account borders on the miraculous.

The night of the fire, Rudy, like many of his neighbors, was awakened by the wind.

"I got up because I heard the wind blowing. The plastic chairs and buckets outside were banging on the ground. I went outside with my flashlight and watched. The wind was blowing strong."

After righting the patio furniture, Rudy returned to bed. Less than an hour later, he received a startling call from a neighbor who lived down the hill from his property.

"She asked me if I could see the fire coming up the hill. I could, and it was way, way too close. She told me, 'I'm leaving, and you should do the same.' I could see the start of the fire from my home."

In the minutes it took for Rudy to assess his situation, it became evident it was already too late for escape. The fire was roaring up his road, and across the valley he could see flames towering hundreds of feet above the hilltops. There was only one way out, and the fire was racing up that escape route, directly toward Rudy's home, which was located on an open, flat section of land ringed by trees. Near the orchard was a meadow about 500 feet from his house.

"I decided to move my rigs—my truck and my car—to the meadow. After that, the flames were right here." Within seconds, the meadow started burning. "The fire raced across the field. It looked like a wave," Rudy said.

Over and over, as Rudy recounts his tale, his ingenuity and resourcefulness come to the fore, saving his life not once but multiple times.

"I knew I had to save my rigs. For some reason, I still had the disc hooked up to my tractor. I made two turns around the rigs and that somehow kept the flames away from the vehicles." Then Rudy looked north. "There were huge flames in the north canyon; it was completely on fire."

Like many rural residents, the Kellys had made preparations for fire. The copious spring on the property meant that Rudy's water tank was full. A hydrant had been installed just a few yards from the house. Rudy knew the drill, and began to wet down as much of the house as he could.

"By then, there were flames in the trees, very close to the house—flames a hundred feet tall. The chicken coop caught fire. Luckily there were no chickens inside. I tried to put out the fire on the coop, and from there I tried to put out the fire near the backup generator on the side of the house. I was running like crazy."
Then something occurred that Rudy will never forget:

"In the middle of all of this, a deer showed up. He just stood next to me. He never ran. He just looked at me, while I was soaking wet. I felt like he was thanking me for trying to save us. He just watched me. I felt like he was asking me: 'What are we going to do?' In my mind, I told the deer, 'I don't know.'"

In minutes, one of Rudy's storage sheds, just a few feet from the main house, caught fire. Extinguishing that fire became paramount.

"I dragged the hose to the shed and put water on both sheds near the house. I could feel the flames by then; could feel the heat. I tried to put water on the roof. Everything was on fire. Everything."

Any firefighter will tell you that dragging a 150-foot, water-filled hose requires incredible strength. Doing it alone, surrounded by flames, is a burden no one should have to endure.

By then Rudy was exhausted, and he collapsed on the ground, but about fifty feet away, he saw a terrifying sight: Flames licked the base of the propane tank. He had to put out that fire at all costs.

"I was stuck. I couldn't move. I tried to walk. I became paralyzed. But I knew I had to protect the house. I started crawling toward the tank. Suddenly I felt something on the ground. I was thinking it was maybe a poison-oak vine, but I knew there was no poison oak that close to the house. I pulled on this vine, used it to drag myself forward till I reached the propane tank. Somehow, I put out the flames with my shoes. That's all I had."

To this day, Rudy has no idea what sort of vine he was pulling, or how he managed to reach the propane tank before it could explode.

The sky was so bright from the fire that no illumination was needed. Searing embers were falling on him. There was no more pressure in the hose line. A long-unused outhouse caught fire only yards from the main house, and then an even more harrowing site unfolded: the roof of his beloved home was igniting.

"I was soaking wet from a leak near the fire hydrant. I grabbed a ladder and climbed on the roof, which is extremely steep and tall. My sweater was soaked. I took off my sweater and managed to beat out the flames on the roof."

Rudy walks to a spot just twenty feet from his front door. "That night, there was a wheelbarrow here. When I climbed down from the roof, the rubber tire on the wheelbarrow burst into flames. How hot does a fire have to be to catch a rubber tire on fire?"

That was the moment when Rudy almost gave up.

"I thought, What's going to be next? Maybe this is my end."

He did a quick assessment of what else he could do. "I still had drinkable water. I had a backpack sprayer. I filled it with drinking water and tried to put out whatever flames I could—a flame here, a flame there, till I used the last drop of water."

There was only one more option left for Rudy: the water in his spring, located about an eighth of a mile from the house.

"When I arrived at the spring, the tank was in flames. I said one word: Shit!" He smiles. To make matters worse, a burning tree had fallen and was blocking access to the spring.

"I got the tractor and five five-gallon buckets and got as close to the spring as I could. I ran to the spring, filled the buckets, loaded them into the tractor, and filled the backpack sprayer with water from the buckets—all night, all morning, and into the rest of the day."

By the following morning, two of Rudy's neighbors showed up.

"They were checking on everyone. We were so happy when we saw each other. They said, 'You made it!' I asked if all of our neighbors escaped. They told me they'd found some of the members of the Shepherd family, and that they didn't all make it out. They didn't know where John Shepherd was. That's when I found out my neighbors below me had also passed away."

Rudy tears up at the memory of that moment.

"They were my neighbors! They lived just over the hill from me. I kept wondering if there was something I could have done, but I know that there's a time when you can only do what you can do."

Rudy continued to deploy his backpack sprayer till late in the day. As the sun set, he finally stopped.

"I started crying. I asked myself, how did I make it? I didn't have an answer to my own question, and I still don't. I sat right here and cried like a baby."

Rudy drives his Arctic Cat to the border between his property and the Shepherds' property. Lifeless trees surround the dirt track, and though birds sing nearby, there is a palpable feeling of sadness and loss that seems to emanate from the earth itself. He heard later that his neighbor, who'd warned him of the fire, barely escaped with her life, half of her car melting as she drove through the flames. "I was so much higher up the road, there was no way I would've escaped." he said.

He points to a dirt path. "This is an evacuation route toward the Shepherds' place. There are two ways to go, but that night the fire was covering everything." He takes the Arctic Cat to the abandoned homestead of his nearest neighbor to the east. "I don't think anyone will ever return here."

After the fire, Rudy went into high gear, clearing back chaparral, cutting down trees, improving signage on his road, mourning his neighbors, and making preparations for the next fire. He put a variety of hose couplings on the hydrant. He bought more tanks, increasing his water storage to 15,000 gallons. He welded the leaks on his water tank near the spring, and cleared his property of every extraneous leaf and twig, creating what any firefighter would define as a model of defensible space. He gave away dressers and beds. "I had a house to sleep in. Others were not so fortunate." He knows now that some of his feverish activity was a way of dealing with the trauma he had suffered. "I can't be around fire anymore, and I don't know if I'll ever feel comfortable around it."

For the first few weeks after the fire, not even a blade of grass grew. But with Spring came a new burst of life. "I wish you could have seen this place this Spring," says Rudy. "Jane spread California poppy seeds. The whole area was blooming. Some trees are waking up and others are dying back. Those Manzanitas? They're not going to make it, but maybe the madrones will."

He harbors some anger for what he had to endure.

"That night, I called 911, right at the beginning of the fire. The person who answered said, 'We'll transfer your call to the fire department.' Once I spoke to them, they said, 'Oh yeah, if you're up there, I don't think anyone is going up there. Do the best you can and try to stay safe. Good luck."

Rudy understands now that no fire chief will put their crew directly into the path of a fire, but it doesn't help relieve the pain of losing his neighbors and nearly his own life. But today, despite repeated entreaties to local fire officials, no one has come to see the improvements he has made to his property- improvements that he feels will go a long way to help others if this happens again.

"Not even now has anyone come to talk to me," he notes.

In addition to making improvements to his property, Rudy has made a few other significant changes to his life. "I'm going to church again, which I'm sure makes my mom happy," he smiles. "The rest of my life is not enough time to appreciate this second opportunity I've been given."

Today, the fences are mended, and Rudy is looking forward to harvesting olives soon. "Last year we harvested 499 pounds." Following the fires, with the fences burnt down, Rudy and the Kellys decided to let the animals have their way with the orchard. "They needed the food more than we did." In his heart of hearts, Rudy likes to think that perhaps one of the animals who enjoyed late-harvest apples following the deadliest fire in Mendocino County's history is the very same deer that provided him with the encouragement, support, and companionship to survive— at the exact moment when all seemed lost.

Uneven Match. Painting by Dell Linney.

Sara's Story
Written by Ree Slocum

At the time of the Mendocino Complex fires, Sara Shepherd, her husband, Jon, and their two children, Kressa and Kai, lived on seventy-six acres off of West Road in Redwood Valley. They'd been homesteading for five years, and had recently completed building their new home. Thankfully it was insured.

Sara recalls the night of the fire: "We were awakened by neighbors who told us the hill was on fire. Phone calls started coming that said, 'I can see fire!' and 'You might think about packing up.' This was the second fire we'd experienced, because in July there was a fire on the Ridgewood Grade on the way to Willits. We evacuated then, so we were prepared, you could say. Our valuables were still packed. We loaded the kids and two dogs and went down the mountain." She stopped to pause and clear her throat. "And we never made it. We evacuated in our two vehicles. My husband was in his pickup, I was in a Honda Pilot with the children, and we hit the wall of fire."

They have a two-mile dirt road. Sara tried to back up the car when they hit the fire wall. After a long sigh, Sara continued, "We had to stop the cars and run up the hill. That's when the panic began…'Run! Run!' was all I could say to the kids—just, 'Run!' We ran up the hill. We just kept running." She paused, and we settled into the silence as we sat with that. "What actually happened after that gets a little blurred for me. Our son, Kai, has asthma, and he was– I could hear his labored breathing, and all I could say to encourage him was, 'Keep going! Keep going!'

"Kai is fourteen– was fourteen, and, um, Jon tried to pull back and stay back with him, and my husband's recollection is different than mine [because I don't know what happened], but he stayed back with Kai. When Kai stopped running, he turned into the flames…that's what he did. Yeah, I think a lot of it was just sheer panic and exhaustion. And I don't remember that happening, that's Jon's recollection. My daughter and I kept running…kept running to a spot in our dirt road we call a fire road because our second escape off the mountain was always to go to the fire road if you can't get down this road." Sara took a deep breath and continued, "But that was engulfed in flames as well, so we were encircled in fire. At that point I think I lost consciousness. We all did. When I regained consciousness, I was on the ground and I called for Kressa, my daughter, and she responded. She was there with me and, um, that's the part I have such guilt, that I couldn't comfort her, couldn't speak to her. All I could say was her name. And she would respond to me and we lay there for what felt like days. It was probably hours." Sara had burns over 60 percent of her body, including around her throat and neck. Even though she thought she was talking, she thinks the burns prevented her from talking with Kressa.

"Our neighbor, Paul, found us, Kressa and me. Jon had gone for help and not said anything. He was able to walk and go down the mountain for help, but Paul brought us water from [our homesite]. The house had burned, but he went back and found water and brought it to us! I remember that cool. It was breathtaking to try to drink it after being burned. And numb! You're so numb you don't really feel the pain of the injuries. What a blessing! Our brains take us to a different spot, I think, to protect us.

"So many things go through your mind. Like when I was lying there waiting for help, um this is an awful part, but I could hear the shrieking of the rats, the animals, the sounds of the forest burning, and feeling like fire was still coming toward us. But, you know, you can't move [and you think], What am I gonna do? And weird things go through your head, like I thought my neighbor started the fire because he'd started a grass fire before. Could somebody do this? Could someone actually do this? I remember Paul being there with us."

Sara remembers Paul using Kressa's cell phone to call for help. Sara thinks Kressa was the one more able to talk. "When Kressa finally gave in to someone's helping...um...she said, 'I'm ready to go to the hospital. I'm ready.' I think another thing when we're in so much shock, when you finally let go, I think you lose consciousness and give in."

After that, Sara recalls being with firefighters: "I remember being on the stretcher. I remember the panting, the labored breathing of firefighters just trying to get me down the

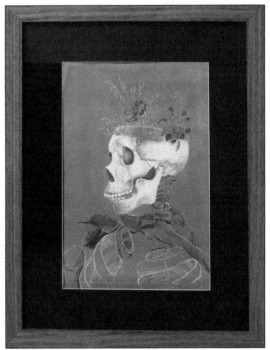

Drawing by Kressa Shepherd.

hill on the stretcher. They had to walk up that two-mile road to get us. Yeah! What a blessing they got there!

"I remember being in the back of a pickup truck for a while. At some point they were able to get me to a truck. I also remember firefighters, I think they were volunteer firefighters. They weren't speaking, and I kept wondering, Why is no one speaking to me? This silence is scary. That's all I remember about that night. The hospital is a whole different experience."

What followed for Sara was being taken by ambulance to the Ukiah Valley Medical Center's ICU, then a helicopter ride to the UC Davis Burn Center. Kressa was taken to Shriner's Children's Hospital in Sacramento, right across from her mother, and Jon went to St. Francis in San Francisco. Sara was in a three-month-long induced coma. She wasn't aware of where the rest of her family was during that time. "Yeah, December I started remembering things again. When I was flat on my back in the hospital bed and I thought, Why can't I walk? Am I ever going to walk again? How'm I going to do this?"

"A lot of people's healing," Sara continued, "or their process of healing, and the children's deaths, happened before I was conscious, so it almost felt like life moved on without me, which it did. And I'm catching up." She's been filling in some of the gaps from other people's memories as to what had happened that night and during the months before she regained consciousness.

Her husband, Jon, who was also badly burned, awoke from his coma sometime in November, and knew about Kai and Kressa before he was able to see his wife in her hospital room.

"I think," Sara said, "we both knew right away that Kai had passed. I don't think we ever forgot that. But Kressa passed the end of October, so Jon knew before I did. We were in different hospitals and we couldn't communicate, so when he finally came to my hospital, he said, 'It's just you and me now.' And in my medical fog I said, 'Oh, we're in heaven?' I thought that meant we were all together now! And what he was really saying was 'The kids aren't here with us.' That was a powerful moment. To try to grasp that, and have my mind wrap around it was, it's still... I'm still in shock. I still feel really numb to it. Unbelievable! Yeah...yeah...."

Mosaic mirror by Sara Shepherd.

Mindi's Story
Written by Carole Brodsky

In Potter Valley, chances are you grew up with every kid in your class, and most likely you knew your teachers and your principal since you were a child. That's the kind of community Mindi Ramos worked in. She was the quintessential small-town principal for the Potter Valley school system, multitasking as school administrator, student counselor, and photographer for the varsity football games. Mindi's husband and their two children, Jack and Betty, were a close-knit family. Her parents, as well as her sister and brother-in-law, Sara and Jon Shepherd, lived nearby. Mindi was a beloved aunt to Sara and Jon's children, fourteen-year-old Kai and seventeen-year-old Kressa, who were close in age to Mindi and Jack's kids.

In early 2017, Mindi and her family lived through a very public, distressing family crisis. Following years of struggle with mental illness, Mindi's husband snapped. Their ten-year marriage collapsed after cascading incidents of domestic violence, restraining orders, and court appearances compelled Mindi to file for divorce. "By summertime, our family was still reeling. We were just beginning to recover. My kids were learning to live beyond the trauma," Mindi explains. She was forced to resign her position as principal and start life anew. Little did Mindi know that in just a few weeks, the strength and courage that carried her through what had been the darkest moments of her life would be required again—this time, to support her family through what can only be described as unspeakable trauma.

Mindi and her children lived in Ukiah. Sara, Jon, Kressa, and Kai lived at the top of a hill in Redwood Valley. Mindi's parents also lived in the valley, but at a different location. On the night of the fire, it was the eerie, late-night gusting of the wind that Mindi recalls.

"The first thing I remember is that it was a really windy night. I didn't think about how it was in Redwood Valley until my mom called me at midnight to tell me about the fire. She said Sara and Jon were evacuating with the kids and were coming down the hill toward my parents' house.

"At that point, my mom's call seemed almost routine," Mindi said. "We'd been through evacuations before, so it didn't seem very unusual." After some time went by, however, Mindi called her mother back to check on the family. "Mom told me she hadn't heard from Sara. That's when I began to worry, but even at that point, we didn't consider that the fire had caught up to them. Everyone was losing phone service, so we just figured they couldn't call out."

Shortly thereafter, Mindi's parents were ordered to evacuate. Her father decided to drive over to the rural road that Sara, Jon, and their kids lived on. He was unable to reach the Shepherd home. "There were EMTs at the bottom of the road who prevented Dad from going up. He pleaded with them, but they didn't want him to be at risk. Without any alternative, my parents got their RV and evacuated to Ukiah."

Then, for the next few hours, the family waited for news from Sara and Jon.

"I think it was about four a.m. when Mom thought we should start checking hospitals. Even then, I remember thinking, Okay, let's just clear out that concern. Everything is probably fine. But everything was far from fine, and in seconds, the family would receive the news that would change their lives forever.

"Mom called the ER in Ukiah. They had admitted a Jon Shepherd. We tried to tell ourselves that Jon Shepherd was a common name, that maybe it was someone else, but just as my mother arrived at the hospital, Sara and Kressa were brought in. My mother heard Sara screaming. This was Mom's daughter—she recognized Sara's voice."

Sara, Kressa, and Jon were immediately sedated. There was no sign of Kai. "It was hard to get any information at all, and they were flown out almost immediately." Then, the daughter of one of the Shepherd's neighbors arrived at the ER. She'd been riding in one of the cars in which Sara and Jon had ridden. "She let us know that Kai didn't make it; that his body was on the mountain. She knew this because her father had found Sara and Kressa."

Mindi pauses. She is crying. She stares into space, and the clatter of the coffeeshop where we're talking suddenly dies away. Time stops. The walls seem to disappear, replaced by the all-too-familiar sights, sounds, and odors of a hospital emergency room. The horror of that moment is still etched on Mindi's face. Then she takes a deep breath. Time starts back up. The chatter of the coffeehouse and the smell of espresso return, and Mindi steels herself for the next part of the story.

"They flew Jon to Bothin Burn Center at Saint Francis Memorial Hospital in San Francisco, and Sara and Kressa were flown to Sacramento. They were admitted to three separate hospitals. Once everyone got flown out, we mobilized and decided our next steps. I packed up my kids and hit the road to Sacramento, to Shriners Hospital for Children, where Kressa had been admitted. It's across the street from UC Davis, where Sara was. Mom and Dad were driving behind me. We figured we could be in one city and help care for two family members. The staff at Shriners were such welcoming, lovely, warm people. They gave us food, somewhere to sit, coloring books for my kids. We needed that. It was really hard to absorb that this tragedy was happening. Then, we kind of collapsed," said Mindi. "Kai was the baby of our family. We were just moving through shock at that point."

Because Mindi was the first adult relative to arrive at the hospital, medical staff asked her to sign admission papers and other documents for Kressa.

"I think an amputation was one of the first procedures I signed for. Then the staff did their best to prepare me to see Kressa. They warned me that she wasn't going to look like herself."

There are no words that can describe a loving auntie entering the ICU to see her niece, a vibrant, artistic young woman who had been burned almost beyond recognition.

"She was burned everywhere. She was mostly wrapped up. Only her fingertips and her face were exposed. They had shaved her head, which was very swollen. I told Kressa that I loved her. I told her that everyone was coming and that everyone was safe, even Kai. I thought, Kai really isn't hurting anymore; he's truly safe."

Then Mindi made a decision, one that she still questions today.

"I told Kressa to keep fighting. And I still feel guilty about that. I still wonder if I should have asked her just to let go."

From that moment, days blurred into nights, and weeks into months.

"I turned into a machine. We lived in hotels, displaced from our homes. Essentially, I lived in Sacramento from the night of the fire until December. I had to remind myself how to sleep, how to breathe, how to eat. Kai was gone. Everyone was burned. I had to provide comfort to my parents and my kids."

Across the street, Sara was in the ICU at UC Davis Medical Center. "She was struggling with anxiety and panic. Her first coherent words were like flashback reactions. She kept repeating, 'Mom, Mom.' At first we thought she was calling for our mom, but that didn't make sense. That's not the person Sara was. Then we realized she was repeating the words of her own children, who must have been calling out for her during their escape."

Over 60 percent of Sara's body had been burned. Jon had been burned over about 50 percent of his body. Both were placed under sedation for a prolonged period, and Mindi couldn't begin to imagine what the future would hold, particularly a future without Kai.

At first, Mindi didn't know how to help her family, other than to be there for them. "The only thing I could think about was to try to be a pillar of strength." As word of the family's tragedy spread throughout the community, Mindi received a flood of messages from friends, well-wishers, and community members. A few calls and a few posts on social media transformed the plight of the family from an exceedingly tragic local news story to international front-page news.

"Everyone wanted to help. People were truly well-meaning, but communicating became exhausting. Once we delegated a few key people whom we kept in contact with, things became a little more manageable," Mindi explained.

Once it was apparent the family would be hospitalized for a significant period, a fundraising drive was set up to help with expenses. "The fundraiser became a way to put out public updates. It was amazing how it touched so many hearts," Mindi said. The family became a focal point for people around the world who were moved by their losses, and the fundraiser was a profound validation of the kindness of strangers.

During the week following the fires, Mindi was contacted by major media outlets.

"I don't remember what the first interview was. I do remember going live on CNN. I had no idea I was going to be on live television until minutes before the interview. It was so strange: There I was, in downtown Sacramento, feeling like I was in the Twilight Zone, giving an interview on CNN, standing in front of a camera, talking to someone I couldn't see."

Along with the area's local paper, the Ukiah Daily Journal, the family's story was featured in dozens of print and online publications, including KQED, The Los Angeles Times, the Press Democrat, the Seattle Times, the San Francisco Chronicle, The Guardian, NBC, the Sacramento Bee, and CBS. All this took place while Sara and Jon, still sedated and recovering at separate hospitals, remained unaware of Kai's death. Amidst the overwhelming sense of loss and uncertainty, there was a ray of hope, as it became clear that Jon and Sara would survive, though both would require extensive support following their discharges from the hospital.

In the weeks to follow, Mindi did not allow herself to think that Kressa would die.

"I told myself, that can't possibly happen; of course Kressa is going to make it." But the prognosis for Kressa had been bleak upon her admission to Shriners, and with every passing day, according to Mindi, her quality of life was deteriorating. "She'd lost both her legs. The doctors weren't sure if she would have any vision or functionality in her hands."

Kressa was on dialysis, and had undergone several surgeries, including skin grafts to her face. She had gone into cardiac arrest and been revived, and had struggled with infection. About three weeks after the fire, physicians told Mindi that Kressa's brain was not functioning. "It was gone. She wasn't reacting to pain stimuli."

It was time to take Kressa off life support. "The staff gave us the time we needed to communicate with family, so everyone could be there before they turned the machines off."

Knowing that Kressa's future would have been filled with profound disability and hardship, Mindi found a small degree of solace knowing that Kressa was no longer suffering. But she had to continue to dive deeper into her own wellspring of endurance and survival, knowing that her sister and brother-in-law would require a monumental measure of support to cope with the loss of their children.

After several more weeks, Jon became stable enough to be moved to Sacramento where he was admitted to UC Davis and reunited with Sara, who remained at Davis for three more months. Jon was discharged two months after his initial hospitalization. They both required months of significant aftercare and return trips to Davis. Sara had to regain her ability to walk and recover from the effects of smoke inhalation. Jon lost the tips of his fingers when his burn grafts failed.

"We learned so much so quickly about the complexities of recovering from burns. The recovery went on for months and months," said Mindi. What the family learned about the loss of their beloved children, grandchildren, niece, and nephew is something so intimate, so tender, and personal that it's best to leave those feelings where they begin and end— within the bottomless chambers of one's own heart.

Mindi notes that the family's first Thanksgiving without Kai and Kressa was spent at Ronald McDonald House in Sacramento. Both the Rotary House and the Ronald McDonald House became like personal sanctuaries. "It was a blessing to be able to stay so close to the family. The staff checked on us, brought us water and snacks, and at the hospitals, we were provided rooms where we could rest together." Mindi notes that she didn't experience the flames of the conflagration. "Because I left for Sacramento, I didn't see the smoke or the scorched landscape. I did see the aftermath—a whole new thing for me. The first time I saw the burn scars it was shocking." She saw the fire's history; how it swirled, tornado-like, onto and around the Shepherd property, blocking their road and cutting off the family's only path to safety.

"It took days and months to piece together what it was like for them trying to come down the mountain," says Mindi.

Mindi and Sara's parents have chosen to let Mindi continue as the family spokesperson. "Mom and Dad are still dealing with grief. They lost a portion of their home, but nothing too serious. They took on logistics after the fire: insurance, banking, document replacement, and everything else. Sara and Jon were unable to participate in that aspect of the recovery, so Mom and Dad did that." Today, Sara and Jon have moved into Ukiah, and their former property has been likened to sacred ground.

Looking back, Mindi realizes that her painful divorce provided the training ground for what was to come. "I had referred to my previous trauma as a blessing disguised as a nightmare that got me to a healthier place. I consider myself lucky that I'd lost my job, because after the fire, I was able to be with my family and support them."

Asked how she copes with the ongoing grief and trauma, Mindi offers some sage advice:

"You have to let the pain come when it comes; to allow each other to collapse in tears when you have to." Her children still miss their only cousins. "My son, Jack, is six. He's very vocal about when his cousins are on his heart and he's feeling very sad. It's important to make it normal to talk about those things."

The family remembers and honors Kressa and Kai in everything they do. "We keep an altar up with their pictures. I'm gratified to have my sister be more of a part of my life. I'm someone who heals through talking and writing, so it was important for me to create a poem." Mindi read her poem at a candlelight vigil that took place in Redwood Valley on the one-year anniversary of the fire.

What has Mindi learned? "What I've learned is to seize joy whenever you can. Life is much too short. Act with love. Tell people you love them. Nothing else is worth it but love.

"Sara and Jon are moving through their first holiday season without their children. Kressa was always very festive. She loved to decorate and make crafts. We're trying hard to hold on to that seasonal tradition. We're seeking joy and living our lives in honor of Kressa and Kai."

Photo by Danny Pardini.

Impermanence and Glory:
Finding the Monks of
Tomki Road after the October Wildfires
Written by Kirsten Ellen Johnsen

I pulled open the heavy wooden door. A cool breeze welcomed us into the dusky interior of the old redwood cathedral on the mountain. In the center of the nave, three offering candles burned upon a small table in a tray filled with sand. Father Damian genuflected before this altar and went to join the brothers singing in the sanctuary. I couldn't believe he was allowing my friend, Joe Rosato Jr., to bring his NBC camera equipment inside the cathedral of the Holy Transfiguration Monastery to film their noontime prayer. The scent of frankincense, soaked into icon-studded walls over many years, wafted over us. It was the first sweet breath I'd breathed in over a week, ever since the fires hit.

Even after the unbelievable happens to you, it's still hard to comprehend. One early morning in October 2017, thousands of people throughout northern California awoke to their worst nightmare come true. A storm of fire, whipped to a devilish fury by rare "Diablo" winds, roared on all sides. People barely had time to grab their loved ones and run. With walls of flame advancing more quickly than the imagination can bear, they panicked—which direction to go? It was survival by wits alone. Some, trapped and overtaken, perished. The inferno was so hot it left behind warped steel.

Joe and I had driven through a landscape of ash for the past few days, seeking to tell the stories of my own home community. Mendocino County's rural tales of midnight flight, heroic struggles, lost lives, homes, and unthinkable destruction were being lost amidst the stories and images of a horror unfolding in the more populated regions closer to the Bay Area. The 30,000-acre Redwood Complex Fire was literally left off the news maps of what was being reported merely as the "North Bay" fires.

Who could really blame them at first—who could have predicted neighborhood after neighborhood of whole city blocks incinerated in a matter of hours by the multiple fires that broke out that night? Downed power lines and blown PG&E transformers were sparked into flame, whirled into a furious firestorm by the intense, dry winds. That's what people were saying. Even department stores and hotels burned down. The destruction was hard to imagine, the images simply mindboggling, but after several days of being ignored by regional and national media we locals got mad. We were suffering too! We too were frantically trying to track down friends, neighbors, family members who'd had to flee in the dark. We too were stunned—once we found them—by their stories of narrow escape.

In any rural area people are deeply networked. Everyone knows everyone, or at least knows someone who does. Over the first few days of the fire, while it still raged through the hills and mountains, threatening more and more neighborhoods, everyone in town realized that every single person knew several others who had barely escaped and lost everything.

Joe is my friend from summer music and dance camp. I know him as a quiet, friendly standup bass player who slips onstage to humbly hold down the bass line during summer dances. He plays a variety of musical styles. He's always wearing his signature cap along with a shy smile and quiet demeanor. I had never thought much about his other life. I was simply relieved that NBC had assigned him to Mendocino County after feeling pressure from so many distraught people trying to get information on the dangers facing their friends and family. Just happening upon Joe's Facebook post mentioning his arrival in my hometown, I messaged him immediately.

In the first week afterward, Mendocino County was in a whirlwind, still scrambling to find relief for evacuees, their pets, and livestock. Dear friends of mine awaited word on their homes and livelihoods left behind as the fire spread. Tales of escape from the firetrap—of people who'd braved the backroads through forests pulsating with fire, or had driven straight through walls of flame in daring feats of rescue—were just beginning to be known. It was the time when the names of those missing for too long were being paired with human remains found in the debris.

Joe lives in San Francisco. He doesn't know Ukiah, Willits, Redwood Valley, or Potter Valley. He doesn't know the tight-knit community connections were built up here over a lifetime living in one place. So I made a few calls. As we drove through Ukiah I pointed out people on the street I knew who had lost everything. In minutes Joe was following several potential story leads.

The first thing I asked Joe in my Facebook message was: "Please help me find our monks!" He must have thought I was crazy. I insisted on describing them to him. "Yes, it's true, we have two monasteries up Tomki Road. They're neighbors. Their adjoining land is nestled at the top of a road that twists between ridges." Tomki Road continues past them, turning into an old road that isn't well known, even to our own residents. The pavement runs out and becomes a four-wheel track that fords several back-country creeks and ultimately leads to the town of Willits, twenty miles north of Ukiah.

"You want cool-looking footage?" I asked Joe. "Let me tell you—a Ukrainian Catholic cathedral tended by gray-clad monks, stained glass windows, and the works—it even has onion domes! And right next door, I kid you not, saffron-robed Buddhist monks meditate in austere halls." I think Joe was, more often than not, simply listening kindly to my raving; lending a sympathetic ear to a stressed-out friend.

The Ukrainian Catholic monks of the Holy Transfiguration Monastery live in spiritual seclusion. They run a small retreat center and offer periodic religious services to the community. Nearby, the Abhayagiri Monastery follows the Thai Forest

Monk tradition of Buddhism. Every week they make alms rounds through Ukiah and Willits, for it is their tradition to receive all of their sustenance from their host community. Sometimes they can be seen walking in meditation along the streets with alms baskets. Offerings made to them are received with blessings bestowed by chants sung in Pali, the Buddha's original language.

"I'm not kidding, Joe," I repeated. For days I'd scanned Facebook for any mention of them during the fires that raged up Tomki Road. Did the monks make it out safely? People shared monk sightings to reassure others. The monks were okay. "I saw some in Willits," one said. "They're staying with friends," another proclaimed. But no one knew what had happened to the beautiful monasteries.

It seemed far-fetched, though, that Joe would be able to find them, even using his magical press-pass powers. The upper part of Tomki Road was under hard closure as firefighters concentrated on defending the homes in the hills. Joe went home after finding other local stories, interviewing brave and beautiful people who faced utter devastation. He brought me to the restricted areas, and while he shot footage, I took arty pictures of the ashen landscape with my iPhone.

When Joe texted me just a couple of days later to tell me his assignment for Ukiah had been renewed, I was finishing a substitute job for the Ukiah Unified School District. It was the kids' first day back to school. In my classroom of thirty fifth graders at the Grace Hudson Elementary School, I asked for a show of hands. Two thirds of the class knew at least one family who'd lost everything in the fires. Half knew more than one family in such a circumstance. One third had direct family members who'd lost their homes. This was how deeply impacted our community had been.

This time driving around with Joe, I didn't let the monk quest go. I met him after teaching school and we began our search. I brought him to the City of Ten Thousand Buddhas, a monastic community located in Talmage, near Ukiah. We went there seeking the Abhayagiri monks who had taken shelter there for the past week. We left them a message at the front desk, and then toured the grounds.

The City has a restaurant, a university, and a very large, ornate, main temple for meditation, ceremony, and dharma talks, all located on the grounds of the old state mental hospital. Governor Reagan had shut it down and released all the patients, and soon after, Hsuan Hua, a Chinese Buddhist monk, purchased it and transformed it into a thriving Buddhist community. Now, flocks of peacocks roam manicured driveways renamed "Bodhi Way" and "Mindfulness Avenue" amidst large statues and images of the Buddha, Kuan Yin, and other deities of the Chinese Zen Buddhist tradition.

I realized how much I took all this for granted as I witnessed Joe being simply floored. He stared amazed at the 10,000 golden statues of the Buddha. Joe has a sweetly irreverent side to his humor. He quipped, "Wow, I guess there must have been a sale!" as he stretched his neck to look at the temple walls that house these icons from floor to ceiling. In actuality, the icons were molded by Hsuan Hua himself.

The next day we drove all the way out Tomki Road. I had called St. Peter's Orthodox Church in Ukiah to ask what had become of the Holy Transfiguration monks, and was told that they'd just returned home. We drove past all the destroyed homes Joe had filmed before. Now that the evacuation order was lifted we could see residents surveying the wreckage of their lives for the first time. Mile after mile revealed an eerie landscape. House foundations had been reduced to ash pits. Blackened stone lawn statues stood among dark-streaked brick chimneys, twisted washing machines, the detritus of dreams and memories. Vehicles had been so utterly gutted by the heat of the fire that windshields had melted in sheets, dripped over what was left of metal dash frames, and pooled into the springs of the seats. Aluminum from melted hubcaps ran in crying silver rivers over the ground beneath twisted gray cars. It was a weeping world, full of palpable sorrow.

Both of us felt hollowed out by these ruined shapes. No words could describe it, and no words needed between us to know we shared the same awe. The landscape of grief was hauntingly, horribly beautiful. We could only be left with reverence in our awareness of profound human suffering in the face of an utterly leveling power of nature. Here and there a lone individual stood staring down her loss, or searching the ground for a trace of his former life. We drove past them up the hill.

The destroyed area thinned, and more green forest became visible. As we drove, I tried to imagine the road on fire as people fled in the dark and smoke. Under the trees the underbrush was swept clean by ash, and here and there were blackened treetops where the flames had climbed into the canopy. We passed a large cement sign to the Abhayagiri Monastery written in Thai and English, and then proceeded several turns to the entrance to the Holy Transfiguration Monastery. There we saw an image of the Blessed Virgin painted in the old Byzantine style, protected by a wooden awning. Around a bend we came upon another signpost. It featured a black silhouette of a dancing devil, replete with horns, bat wings, forked tail, and cloven hooves, inside a red circle with a diagonal slash indicating that no devils were allowed here. I cracked up laughing. Someone here had a sense of humor!

The parking lot was very still. Joe exhaled, "Wow," as he saw the gated entrance and cathedral for the first time. Over the gate, hung with lichen, an Orthodox cross topped the bell tower. A wooden onion dome perched upon the stained-glass steeple of the church. A large gold onion dome graced the entry gate. The monastery was safe.

"Yes, it's beautiful," I breathed. I'd been here before, for services and a school field trip. This time, however, something else caught my eye. The small church was roofed with redwood shakes. A work of art, love, and devotion, each shingle carefully overlapped to create a scalloped surface, offered innumerable air-filled crevices for the embers that surely had flown over it all week. It was the most flammable building I'd seen all day. How in the world had it survived?

Yet here it was, and here we were, surrounded by the peace of the day, overlooking the forest. The place seemed empty. I led Joe through the gates. We peered into empty windows to view rows of rosaries and icons for sale, but saw no one. "Do you think anyone's here?" Joe asked, a few paces behind me.

"It can't hurt to knock," I said. I approached the dining hall and tapped on the door.

Ah, there were voices. Did they hear me? I knocked again. After my third try I heard a distinct, "Yes, yes, I'm coming," and the door opened. A small-statured man stood there. He had a wispy, grizzled beard and twinkling blue eyes behind his spectacles. He was all smiles.

"Welcome, welcome! Thank you so much for coming!" he crooned, stepping aside to usher us into the large hall. He assailed us with his warmth. "I am Father Damian! How are you?"

This question has echoed all around town of late. Once a polite formality, now it is spoken with new sincerity between both old friends and perfect strangers. Askers hang on the answer: "I'm okay, but my father-in-law, my friend, my daughter, my grandmother, barely made it out, thank God for their neighbor who..." Or simply, "All that matters is that I made it out. I'm alive, and I have my family." I assured him I was fine, but that of course I had many, many friends who'd lost everything.

Father Damian continued, "Can I get you anything? Tea? Coffee?" Joe, timidly entering behind me, politely declined, but I, a mythologist, gleefully accepted. "Thank you so much, please, yes, black tea!" I answered. I accepted the role of the sacred guest, a tradition as old as civilization the world over.

Father Damian consented to an interview with Joe for NBC, even though it interfered with his noontime prayer. Brother Seraphim came down the dirt road to ring the great bell. Joe was eager to film the ringing so he could have sound to interlace with imagery for his report. The abbot joked with Brother Seraphim that he'd be a Hollywood star, and the brother smiled with the preoccupied expression of one whose life is devoted to eternal matters, amused at such temporal silliness.

Returning to the dining hall, Father Damian pulled out some benches from around one of the wooden tables. It was a large rectangular room, decorated with Catholic iconography and warmly lit by large windows looking over the forested ridge. His eyes sparkled, and his ruddy face beamed as he told his tale. He described how the flames rising from the valley looked like the sun coming out of the earth itself, as if the world had turned upside down. He had rung the bells to alert the monks in their cloisters scattered through the woods. Unfortunately, they thought it was another call to prayer, if perhaps a bit early. "I really do need to rethink our alarm system," he mused with a grin.

One monk drove toward town to see if he could find a way out for the brothers, but soon realized there would be no escape that way as all kinds of animals—dogs and cats and horses—ran toward him from a wall of flames. The monk, ever the servant to God's creation, stopped to pick up a few small animals in his car before returning to the monastery to tell the monks the news—they were trapped.

Knowing they couldn't drive out the back way in their two-wheel-drive Priuses, they stayed in the chapel and prayed. All night long, while the fire raged below them, they worshipped and wondered. They debated what they should do if it got really bad. Burn with the cathedral, or sit in the weed-thickened pond?

"I thought I'd rather die of an algal infection from the pond than burn to death," said Father Damian.

At about noon the next day a team of firefighters drove into their parking lot and urged them to leave. They were then escorted out the main road, passing scenes of destruction so disorienting that Father Damian lost his sense of direction. For a week they were housed by parishioners of St. Peter's to await news on the fate of their monastery.

Father Damian spoke with humility, compassion, and touching grief for the fate of his neighbors who had lost their homes, lost even their loved ones. His irrepressible humor had Joe and me in stitches. Joe, raised Italian Catholic, seemed particularly charmed by the abbot's accessibility and wit. He described how impressed he was with his visit to the City of Ten Thousand Buddhas. "They really do have 10,000 of those," Joe mused. "That's not just an idle boast!"

Father Damian, quick to respond, leaned forward conspiratorially. "It's an idol boast!" he punned. We just about fell off our chairs, trying to choke back our laughter. Joe and I were warmed through by this beautiful, genuine, human connection with a spiritual man who was just as deeply affected by this tragedy as we were.

I don't remember how we were invited into the cathedral for the prayer service. It just seemed the natural next thing to do. How could anyone not pray at this time, for grief, for gratitude? So there we were, in the nave of the cathedral, lit by flickering candles and colored sunshine through stained glass, breathing frankincense. As we listened to the exalted tones of prayer in three-part harmony, Joe looked over his shoulder at me from his camera tripod with a huge grin and a thumbs-up. I smiled back through my tears.

The traditional Ukrainian Catholic service was sung in English, praising the eternal glory of God. To my surprise, Father Damian suddenly began intoning an inspired, spontaneous prayer for all survivors of the fires, asking the Lord to bless and keep the hearts and souls of those who had died; and for those who had lost everything, to help them and their relatives to come though this hardest of times. Tears coursed down my cheeks. I lit a candle to join the sand tray with those of the three praying monks.

As we left, the father spoke of his neighbors, the Abhayagiri Buddhists. It was lucky, he thought, that over the past few years the two monasteries had struck a deal to clear the forest of underbrush along their shared borders. "They can't kill anything," he said, "so we cut the brush, and they chop it up for us!" He described the friendship they've negotiated. "We've agreed not to talk about ecumenical stuff," he explained. "We just don't understand each other." He asked us if we'd seen their "No devils allowed" sign on the driveway entrance, and went on to confide that his Catholic Brothers were concerned that the Buddhists would think the sign was referring to them, but that instead the Buddhists loved it, and wanted one of their own!

Joe and I drove away, giddy. We descended through the acres of charred homes. Our elation from spending the day in communion with a gentle, spiritual man who had endured so much with his brethren, and who still enfolded us in his prayers, sobered as we witnessed once more the drawn faces of people surveying the ashes of their ruined lives.

Suddenly from the blackened forest I saw a flash of saffron. "There they are!" I cried. Joe pulled over. "Is that them?" he queried.

"Absolutely. That's Abhayagiri."

The Buddhist monks were walking together amidst the wreckage of a home. A few wandered the gray landscape, but soon they all gathered in a circle and began to chant. I watched Joe hurriedly unpack and set up his camera equipment. He was focused and intent, and I smiled at him. See? Wasn't I right about this? I thought smugly. And I felt the joy of living in such a wonderful, special community.

I stood a respectful distance from the chanting with my hands in prayer at my chest, feeling my own gratitude mixed with grief. My mind swirled, unable to contain it all. How can all of this be—such loss and such love, all rolled into one, huge, confusing experience? Through the gathered saffron robes I could see a woman standing in the center of the circle; she held the statue of a Buddha and wept. I thought of all of my dear friends with no home to go to now, who woke up in the night to rouse children, thankful for the one thing that matters in all of this world: love. The chanting rose and fell under black trees. Here, maybe, the healing could begin.

After he'd finished the blessing ceremony, a senior monk approached us with the easygoing gait and open countenance of a man whose life is becalmed by dedicated spiritual practice. Again, we were the sacred guests, welcomed to the fold. The Abhayagiri monks were just now returning to their monastery; would we like to accompany them? We spoke with the abbot, Ajahn Pasanno, who greeted us with warmth and curiosity.

By this time it was Joe who seemed crazed and on a mission. I could hardly communicate with him as he single-mindedly sped back up Tomki Road to turn in at the large cement sign, ABHAYAGIRI. He set up his camera in just the right vantage point to film their return. He knew exactly what angle he wanted.

The monks took it all in stride, focused purely upon the blessing of their return to their homes. Piling out of cars in their parking lot, they rewrapped their robes and began to slowly walk up the hill toward their unscathed buildings. They had recently finished a remodel of their entire grounds to include a larger meditation hall and a commercial kitchen. The structures were impressive. The stark architecture in an austere style was so new that the cement pathways connecting the buildings ran through incomplete irrigation for unfinished landscaping. They had to leave all this development to escape in four-wheel-drive vehicles out the back end of Tomki Road toward Willits, and for a week didn't know if they would return to any monastery at all. I wondered how they'd managed to evacuate twenty-five monks who by traditional practice are restricted from driving.

Joe and I walked respectfully behind the monks as they slowly sang their way home. Ajahn Pasanno led them directly into their new meditation hall to lead a chant of blessing before a white stone statue of the Buddha. I sat on the side bench next to a relieved, proud mother of one of the monks and felt myself relax into an inner space. I wish I could say I felt an inner quiet, but my head was buzzing. My heart and mind still leapt with excitement and confusion, grief and joy, horror and wonder. As I focused on relaxing my breathing, I noticed the contrast of feeling between these very different styles of prayer. Here, I deepened into what I could manage of a moment-to-moment awareness. I felt my body integrate the sense of the previous Catholic prayer into this Buddhist moment.

There was an ironic balance to all of it. The flammable Orthodox Catholic chapel perched in ephemeral beauty to praise an eternal God. Its scented sanctuary lifted my spirit to heights of wonder. The Abhayagiri meditation hall sat square, solid, and strong in the face of impermanence. In its refuge I sought my center, breathing into simple acceptance.

I've been blessed to travel the world, and in my journeys have visited many sacred sites. I've wandered the stupas of Borobudur in Indonesia, visited the Temple of the Emerald Buddha at the Golden Palace in Bangkok, witnessed indigenous cremations in Tana Toraja, Sulawesi, and participated in a Baruk dance in Bali. I've found eternal beauty in the ancient pagodas of Pagan in Myanmar, and visited the Byzantine Temple of the Hagia Sofia as well as the Blue Mosque in Istanbul. I have joined with Druids in dawn ceremony inside Stonehenge, and prayed in the ancient aisles of the Lutheran church of my ancestral forebears in Romania. I've sat atop Mayan temple ruins, lost in thought on cultures gone by, and honored the ancestors of the land at local Pomo ceremonies.

To seek and find the monks of Tomki was as powerful as any peak experience. From the burnt neighborhoods of Redwood Valley to the spiritual sanctuaries of the ridgetop, I was hallowed by this immense reality of loss. From the lowland cremation grounds to the mountain heights of prayer, I prayed supplication to the omnipotent force of God beyond all comprehension, then settled into simple loving-kindness in acknowledgment of the impermanence of all worldly phenomena. My heart had been dipped in pain, wrung by compassion, released into glory, and salved by presence.

Even though my mind couldn't stop whirling like a fire tornado, something inside me that remained somehow in stillness offered this one wish for all the people traumatized by the northern California fires: that we may each find our own way to peace.

Joe's gone home now, back into the city world of cultural news reporting, and hopefully a few good music sessions. I am here in Mendocino County, learning how to help rebuild my community with my dear old friends and many new ones.

Among these new friends I count the abbots of Tomki: Father Damian and his friend and neighbor, Ajahn Pasanno. I give thanks for their fortune and look forward to the spiritual solace they offer.

Joe's report can be viewed on his NBC reporter page. After he had rushed to town to upload it, he mentioned one funny detail he'd noticed with his musician's ear. The chanting of the Buddhist monks and the prayers of the Catholic monks were in the same key. Their voices blended beautifully.

A Tree to Remember. Painting by Rose B. Easterbrook.

Fire Survivor Ensemble

Fire Survivor Ensemble

Created and directed by Ellen Weed
Script edit by Mary Buckley

Featuring:
Nori Dolan
Clint Hudson
Jaelin Mosscarille
Cathy Monroe
Mary Monroe
Charlotte Scott
Ross Walker

With live music by Clint Hudson, Kim Monroe,
Bill Taylor, Ross Walker, and Mary Buckley

"Wildfire Haiku" throughout script by Cathy Monroe

Music: "October 8–9," "Mendocino Coast Storm"
and "Midnight Malarkey" keyboard compositions by Bill Taylor

"Scorched Earth" song by Mary Buckley

First performed at Ukiah Senior Center, Ukiah, California
September 19, 2018,
and Redwood Valley Grange, Redwood Valley, California
October 20, 2018

Act I

BILL TAYLOR: Preshow original keyboard instrumental music: "October 8–9"
KIM MONROE: Homeless by Paul Simon
CAST: Enter/introduce selves and take seats
NORI: "Improvisational Story Dance"

MARY: Our stories intersect like a flood in the mountains—
Rivulets cascading, crisscrossing, rushing down the mountain, then slowing…
Confusion, cars milling about—eddies of uncertainty, unsure which way to go…

CLINT: Since I was eleven years old, I've never lived in any place for very long.
It was unusual for me to stay in one place for more than a year. So in 2002 I was
between houses, and most of my belongings were stored in my shop in town, or in
my truck. During this time, I came to Rancho Mariposa to help finish a yurt. While
I was away one weekend, my shop burned down. I suddenly found myself without
most of my tools—or many possessions at all—but at least I still had a job.

Over the years, I lived on the ranch, and its people became my friends and my
family and my community. I got to know the land and the people. The more time
went by the more I began to see how special a place and how uplifting a community
the Rancho Mariposa is, and I began to fall in love with it.

MARY: We celebrated our youngest son Wesley's thirty-second birthday at
Rancho Mariposa on the night of Sunday, October 8. Roasted veggies, barbecued
chicken, Boston cream pie—I'd prepared food all day in my tiny yet well-equipped
kitchen.

We ate at the kitchen table, on the beautiful indigo tablecloth that my nephew,
Ian, had brought back from China. We ate from the blue plates that Ruth Easterbrook had made when she was in college. A bottle of wine sat on a Jan Hoyman
plate so the wine wouldn't stain the tablecloth. The house was filled with warmth
and humor, as it usually was for family gatherings.

CHARLOTTE: I had a great weekend with my family. On Friday evening, after
picking up my teenage stepchildren, I gave my stepdaughter, Izzy, an early fifteenth
birthday present—a new ukulele. Izzy also agreed to go with me to my favorite yoga
class on Saturday morning, followed by a blissful lunch in the Jyun Kang restaurant
at the City of Ten Thousand Buddhas.

On Sunday, we reveled in leisure at home—I made a huge Italian dinner, and
we all went to bed looking forward to an extra day off from work and school (the next
day was a Monday holiday for most of us). We talked about possibly making a trip to
the Mendocino Coast or Santa Rosa.

JAELIN: On Saturday, after the Farmers Market in Ukiah, I left my husband, Bill Taylor, at home in Redwood Valley to return to my sanctuary—my artist residence—in Willits. I was extremely grateful for the opportunity to work without interruption, and to prepare for a fundraising party and sing-along to help restore our grounds, which had burned up in the July 2017 Grade Fire.

We'd had yet another fire close to our house only a week after the Grade Fire, so I left for my studio feeling guilty for leaving Bill with a charred landscape and copious amounts of restorative work still to be done.

ROSS: October 8, 2017 was my seventieth birthday. I spent it with family, going to the corn maze in Petaluma, then out to eat. We arrived home pretty tired.
As a treat for my wife, Charlotte, myself, and our dear nine-year-old grandson, Ari, we kept him with us after the family gathering so he could spend the night at our place. Ari went right to sleep in the guest bed, and Charlotte and I were fast asleep in our room in no time.

CATHY: On Sunday evening, October 8, I dropped off my friend Helen at her house after attending a naturalist conference in the Pepperwood Preserve north of Santa Rosa. We both noted the strange, swirling wind twisting the leaves in the oaks overhead—the kind of wind that precedes a weather change—maybe, we hoped, the long-awaited first rains.

On a walk that day, we had discussed how parched the ground gets that time of year, and the danger of fire in such a tinder-dry landscape. In less than twelve hours this same wind would blow firestorms that devastated Pepperwood Preserve

Photo by Cathy Monroe.

and destroyed both Helen's and my homes in Redwood Valley. It would be the second time I lost my home there, after a structure fire in 2007.

CLINT: In May 2007, a loud boom! awakened me, and I saw a pillar of smoke to the south. Cathy Monroe's house was burning. It was devastating. Less than a week later, Cathy asked if I would be a part of the rebuild. I agreed on the spot, and during that process I felt my respect and appreciation for the community grow again. I also bonded with Cathy over both of us dealing with loss from fire.

In the last year before the Redwood Complex Fire, my life expanded and changed in many ways, and the ranch was my rock to stand on. It helped me to better become myself and feel safe.

On the night of the fire, my world could not have been better—nothing seemed out of place, except maybe how good I felt. I was reveling in the company of a lovely lady I'd recently met. The evening was enchanted, and the dryness of the air and the unseasonable wind were barely noticeable.

NORI: The day before the fire was a hot one! The wind howled that afternoon and into the evening. I spent the day reorganizing my place, and when I went to bed I noticed a dozen or so wine bottles near my bedroom doorway. I heard branches falling and pinecones cracking against the roof as I lay in bed. I was fearful of a tree falling on the house on this stormy night, but somehow the wind lulled me in an almost hypnotic way, and I fell into a deep sleep.

JAELIN: Bill and I talked on Sunday afternoon. "There's a red-flag warning," Bill said in a solemn voice. There was no way I wanted to experience another night like the Grade Fire in July—watching helplessly from below, stopped by firefighters as our beloved land burned, bright and hot, with Bill up there alone, doing all he could. No—my husband, my hero, my partner—I needed to be there by his side, fighting fire if we had to. "I'm coming home, Bill," I said.

I could tell by the tone of his voice that he was very relieved. I drove home and did normal things. Neither of us really expected a fire; we just wanted to make sure we were at the same place if that occurred.

At seven o'clock, while I was making dinner, the winds were hot and howling. Things rattled, and the wind chimes and moving parts clanked more than tinkled—raucous, in fact, and very disturbing.

Later that night, Bill and I fell asleep in each other's arms—glad to be home and in the same place.

CHARLOTTE: I'm a light sleeper and experience insomnia. On Sunday evening, I lay in the dark in our bedroom and listened to the sweet sounds of snoring children throughout the house. I gazed out our large bedroom bay window with its view of the eastern hills between Tomki and Potter Valley and a wide sky, often full of stars.

Short bursts of wind tumbled from the western ridge just above and behind our house, through the canyon below us and down into the valley. I saw the oak branches outside our window move furiously; then there was a sudden calm. It was early Monday morning, about 12:40. Something about that stillness made me more alert. Instantly, the sky above the eastern hills came aglow with an orange light.

My first thoughts turned not to wildfire but confusion—for a split second I thought I was witnessing something celestial. I yelled for Tom to wake up. He was in a deep slumber and I had to shake him a bit: "What is that? What's going on?" Almost immediately, we both saw bright, tall flames at the peak of the eastern hills, and exclaimed, "Fire!"

We got out of bed and I turned on the computer to see if we could find anything on the CAL FIRE incident page or on social media. I saw nothing about the fire, so I started to phone my neighbors. The Monroes' son, Eli, answered, and said he was on the other line with his younger brother, Wesley, who had just called to warn them. I said, "I figured you guys don't have the unobstructed view I have." Eli must have walked outside and gotten a better view of the fire then, because I heard him say, "Oh, wow!"

MARY: Exhausted by our full day, I'd fallen into a deep, restful sleep, so when the phone rang at 12:58 a.m., I thought, Who the heck is calling Eli at this time of night? Our middle son, Eli was living in the cabin next door. I just rolled over and went back to sleep.

A few minutes later, Eli came running upstairs and said, "Mom! Dad! There's a big forest fire burning along the ridge. That was Wes, and they're watching it burn from Potter Valley."

I still get breathless each time I think about that moment, that phone call, and stepping out on the deck to look out across Tomki Road to the east. "Oh, shit!" The entire ridge was a wall of flame, roaring across the canyon—ferocious, whipping, sudden.

Back inside, I scanned our room, wondering what to pack. I was stunned—and somewhat in denial—so I went out and took one more look to confirm the danger. The flames already seemed bigger and louder. A newspaper article I read later said that the fire was moving the length of a football field every three seconds—a hundred feet a second! As I watched it start to burn down the canyons, I definitely started to feel panicky!

I grabbed my overnight bag, threw in some clothes, a couple pairs of comfy pants, a cashmere sweater—why not all three of them?—my toothbrush, hairbrush, and my favorite old orange comb. Why didn't I grab my camera? It was sitting right there. Or the box of photos I had sorted—all the best of our family vacations from when the kids were little? I was calm enough to grab my computer and iPad.

Meanwhile, Eli grabbed the "fireproof" safes. His girlfriend, Ana, remembered that, during the Grade Fire a few months earlier, I'd told her that if I had to save only one of my paintings it would be the one I did of my husband, Kim, and our eldest son, Ben, walking down a ranch road on a drizzly fall day. Ana grabbed that painting, then she and Eli went to wake up the neighbors.

Ana stumbled through the dark to Kevin and Nicole's, shouting "Fire!" till they awoke. At first they were confused, not realizing how late it was, and invited her in for a social visit. "No!" Ana said. "Fire!" Then Kevin ran to wake Cathy, Ross, and Charlotte.

ROSS: The next thing I remember after I went to sleep is hearing our neighbor, Kevin Reilly, shouting outside our house: "Fire! We have to get out!" Kevin is a long-time trusted friend and no alarmist, so I knew it must be serious business.
It was only five minutes from hearing him shout till we were in the car.

The fact that Ari was there was about all I could think of, and Charlotte was right in sync with me. We weren't about to wait a moment more than it took to get dressed and go. As I lifted Ari from his bed to wake him and tell him what was happening, I breathed a sigh of relief, as he understood right away that there was an emergency and no time to waste.

I looked at my laptop and then considered getting documents, like our passports, but my brain registered confusion at the thought of taking time to consider what else—besides us—was most important to save, so I just focused on getting us dressed and out of there.

I pulled on a pair of short pants and made sure that Ari had a long-sleeve shirt and shoes on. I took my cell phone and wallet, Charlotte took hers, and we were out

View of the fire from Road I at 1:30 AM. Photo by Shari Bainbridge.

the door. As I think back on it, grabbing my laptop, our passports, and a few other documents would have taken maybe a couple of minutes, but that just wasn't what seemed important at that moment.

CATHY: mid night orange glow
all along the ridge line
flames roaring down

A bit before one a.m., a phone call from my nephew, Eli, awoke me. Eli said, "Go outside and look at the sky to the east."

A huge fire was headed our way from Potter Valley, and we needed to get out! I called my brother, Tim Easterbrook, to rouse his family, and quickly dressed as I watched the flames crest the length of the ridge, towering above the tree line. I was horrified to see the flames dive down the mountainside. Other fires I'd seen would linger on top, barely venturing down. This was different—a real inferno!

Then someone barged in my door. It was my neighbor, Kevin, making sure I was alerted before he dashed on to someone else. Before leaving, I needed to find Sarah Nielson's phone number and let her know that there was no time to evacuate our horses. I knew she was very attached to her mare, Wildfire, who boarded at my barn, and I didn't want her to foolishly try to reach the horses. I told her I'd open the gates and hope for the best.

As I drove down to the barn, my dog beside me, I noticed that my mouth had gone completely dry—cotton-mouth—though I felt calm and alert. When I opened the gates, Sarah's horse and my new mustang mare were curious about my mid-night appearance. They gently greeted each other. I left them in the dark, free but unaware of the approaching danger.

Sarah Nielson later said: Within fifteen minutes of getting the call from Cathy— the worst phone call of my life—my husband, Alex, and I were in Redwood Valley, trying to reach our sweet horses. At the East Road bridge, flames were blowing sideways across the road. It was a true firestorm: The wind whipped up the smoke so all you could see was a wall of flame, and falling trees or branches knocking down power lines on the road. It looked and felt like any vision I'd ever had of hell. I was going to try to drive through the flames, but my husband persuaded me otherwise. If he hadn't, I don't think we'd have made it out alive. I began to believe my horse was dead.

CLINT: At one a.m. or thereabouts, I was drifting into blissful sleep when I heard loud footsteps and a familiar voice calling my name. Eli Monroe, Kim and Mary's second son, was yelling that fire was on its way and we all had to leave right now. Eli is somewhat of an accomplished prankster, and at first I was a bit annoyed and didn't accept that he was actually saving my life. As I heard him get into his car and speed away, I walked out my door and stepped into the field in front of my house. First I felt the hot wind from the south on my face; then I saw the orange glow on the horizon.

In that moment I knew this was no prank, and it was time to run. I rushed back inside and informed my friend that we had to go—right now! I grabbed my guitar and a bag of dirty clothes that I'd put by the bedroom door, and told my dog to "load up" into my truck. My friend had her own car, and we both sped away into a dust cloud stirred up by other vehicles that had left before us.

CHARLOTTE: After talking with Eli, I furiously made calls and sent texts to all the other neighbors I could find in my contacts list. I recall thinking, "Everyone else can't see what I see—what if they don't wake up?!" I jumped back on the CAL FIRE website—nothing yet!

We got the children to wake up and put shoes on, and I got my prepacked bag of important paperwork (packed from the previous fire warning a few months earlier)—passports, birth certificates, titles, and jewelry. I threw in clothes for the little kids, and all of my best work clothing. We filled a water bottle for each of us, and I prompted the teenagers to hurry into my Volvo.

I texted my brother that we would need to stay at my mom's house in Ukiah, where he was housesitting, and told him we were on our way.

I knew Tom wouldn't leave with us; he had refused to leave during the last fire scare. He had built this house, and his whole identity is tied to this property. I knew he would be determined to save the property, since we had no insurance or savings.

ROSS: no time to lose
evacuation hustle
keys lost in trunk

Escaping from our house meant driving toward the fire. Half a mile or so along our driveway, heading toward Tomki Road, we drove into billowing waves of hot wind, with cinders blowing into our windshield, and we could hear a roar in the distance.

The roar grew louder as we headed south on Tomki. And as we approached West Road, the tree canopy opened, and we could see a wall of flame ahead. It became obvious that continuing in that direction was a very bad idea.

I knew the back road north, thru the nine creek crossings to get to Willits, and heading that way seemed the only rational thing to do. I told Charlotte we should head north, and she was completely in agreement. Once I turned around, I felt pretty safe. I knew where the fire was; I knew the route to escape; and I knew we could do it.

As we retraced our route back up Tomki, there was a group of half a dozen vehicles pulled over to the side of the road, obviously trying to figure out what do. I stopped. I saw my neighbors Kim and Mary Monroe. I shouted that the West Road route to the freeway looked very dangerous, and that we were heading north. A woman I didn't recognize in one of the vehicles became hysterical, saying you couldn't drive out that way. I told her that it could be done—and that was what we were about to do. And we left.

MARY: Shoes on, out the door... Kim headed down to the shop where he had parked his car. I drove by him, and then drove by our neighbors Andy and Neda, who were carrying things out to their car. I waited for Kim at the bottom of the road, but he didn't show. So I circled back up again, and just as I got to the shop he zoomed out; he had returned for his keys. I sped after him, and passed Andy and Neda again. "See you at Eagle Peak School!" I called out.

Little did I know that West Road was already on fire, and we couldn't go out that way. Little did I know that Andy had dropped his car keys in the dark, and wouldn't be able to leave until about fifteen minutes later. Little did I know that Charlotte and Jan's escape would get blocked by a flaming fallen tree.

I just followed Kim out our mile-long dirt driveway. At first we were so sure where we'd be going—I had told Andy and Neda we'd see them at the school. So we turned right and drove south on Tomki until—BAM! We ran into an eddy of uncertainty at Jimmy's bridge—cars circling like ants on a crumb, the sky red and aglow before us, the unmaintained Tomki behind us. Ross and Charlotte and Ari came zooming back toward us, out of the glow. They stopped and I shouted out the window, "Where are you going?"

ROSS: "It's on fire out there! We're going up Tomki."

MARY: "Up Tomki?"

ROSS: "Well, we can't escape that way—it's all on fire out there!"

MARY: That galvanized the jam; Kim and I turned around and went back up to the end of our driveway where, again, a bunch of cars and people were milling about. Kim got in with me because he realized his car was just about out of gas. Meanwhile, Andy and Neda were still way back up the drive, searching for the car keys that had been dropped in the dark. Thankfully, we later learned that they did make it out by taking West Road—but in a terrifying shower of flying embers and falling, burning logs.

Meanwhile, Ross, Charlotte, and Ari intrepidly flew on up Tomki, like an arrow sure of its path. Eli had warned several neighbors and was about to drive out in his really old Honda Civic. His girlfriend, Ana, yelled, "Eli, no—take the expensive car!" They pulled up next to us in our RAV4. Again I questioned the choice to go up Tomki. Eli said, "Don't worry, Mom, I've driven this road hundreds of times. Just follow me!"

We all turned into a snaky caravan, twisting up the road, breathlessly dipping down and around, into and out of nine creek crossings on the unmaintained part of Tomki Road. I just followed Eli, heading to Willits.

CATHY: It's less than a mile down our driveway to Tomki Road. From the long dirt driveway I could see other car lights. It looked like all of our ranch community was on the move. The plan was to go south on Tomki about a mile, to the junction with West Road, and to meet at Eagle Peak School, but at the end of the driveway we could see the bright glow south of us as well as to the east. Embers swirled overhead. I couldn't see the flames, but others who had ventured south verified that the exit in that direction was on fire. We realized that we'd have to take Tomki Road north to Willits, over fourteen miles of rugged dirt road with lots of precarious, rutted creek crossings.

Our exodus north felt like something out of The Twilight Zone—a strange midnight caravan churning dust through a narrow tunnel of headlight beams through the dark. I watched the cars in front, each dipping down into the pits of the boulder-strewn creek crossings, wondering if my new low-slung Chevy Volt could miraculously make it, as had the Prius ahead. We had expected to be evacuating on regular paved roads, not venturing onto rough back roads!

The KZYX DJ on the car radio kept begging for someone to call in with news about what was going on in Redwood Valley, but no one did, so he was left in the dark along with us—not knowing that the fire was not chasing us north but had raced across the valley to thwart us instead on Highway 101, south of Willits.

CLINT: As we reached the end of the driveway, everything seemed frantic. Many neighbors were in their cars, some getting out and standing by open car doors. Joseph Easterbrook said, "Don't go that way," motioning behind him to the south. "It's already burning—no way through." This meant north was the only option. My friend climbed into my truck because she had doubts that her tiny low-to-the-ground car would make it on the fourteen miles of rough unpaved roads. We pulled out and fell into line with all the other people making their way to safety. I had never been part of an exodus before, but that's what it was.

NORI: night convoy flees fire
dusty twilit creek crossings
DJ pleads for news

Bang! Bang! Bang! was the next thing I heard after I fell asleep. Charlotte Healy, my landlady at the time, was at my door, saying, "There's a fire and we might have to leave!"

I said, "Where?" and she asked if I wanted to go see. I said yes, and off we drove, north on East Road.

I was in a daze, barely awake, when I saw flames coming over the hills from Potter Valley above Barra Vineyards. I will never forget the look of those flames—waking in the haunting middle of the night to a dragon's tongue of fire snaking over the hills to try to catch me in my sleep.

Charlotte said, "Oh, it's closer!" I said, "We need to go back." Once home again, we both started to pack our cars. To begin with, I was very methodical: I grabbed some important papers, pulled out my backpack, put in my laptop, cords, phone, and even the Apple streaming box for my TV. I started to pack clothes—boots, tennis shoes, sandals. I grabbed seven shawls—two of them from my grandmother—a bunch of scarves, and most of my jewelry.

Charlotte needed some help getting Cinnabar, her horse, who was now in the trailer, hooked up to her truck, so I helped her and then headed back into my place. I glanced out my sliding glass door toward the northwest. To my surprise, there were flames in the valley, now coming right toward me. At that moment, I freaked out—I knew this place would soon be toast. I began to move quicker.

Close by, I heard propane tanks explode. The fire was getting closer! I passed the wine bottles and thought, I'm going to want some wine, and so are other people, so I grabbed eight bottles. I was drawn to what was local; little did I know that Backbone Winery would be burned to a crisp and that the Frey Winery would sustain major damage.

All of a sudden, Jini arrived with Carlos, dropping him off to drive Charlotte's car out so that Charlotte could drive the truck and horse trailer. Jini had been trying to reach me, but my phone ringer was off. I paused at the end of the driveway. Smoke was in the air, and the smell of burned forest and structures stuck with me as I drove, in a daze, south on East Road. I was in shock. I now regret that I didn't think to honk my horn to alert neighbors who weren't yet awake.

CHARLOTTE: As we left, we felt that we were well on our way to safety—we were more worried about leaving Tom behind. I sped down our twisty three-mile dirt road as quickly as I could. I remember listening to KZYX and yelling at the radio, "Why is this crappy music still on, but nothing about the fire?!"

Halfway down the driveway, we suddenly saw that the fire had reached Tomki Road—something we hadn't been able to see from above—but we couldn't tell yet whether it had crossed Tomki. I just kept barreling down the harsh, bumpy road, but I began to become even more nervous, and very afraid, because soon I could see that the fire had crossed Tomki. I started laying on the car horn, because I didn't know yet whether Jan Hoyman or her renters would be awake, and as we raced by her place I saw that both of her vehicles were still there. I remember thinking, I can't stop and run in to wake her, because I have these kids in the car. I remember shaking and crying at this point.

As we raced around the turn below Jan's house, Izzy and I gasped. We could see fire throughout the open field, and tall pine trees blazing fifty feet in the air on the side of the driveway ahead. I remember thinking, We just have to keep going, and saying to the kids, over and over, "Everything will be okay!"

Just before the end of the driveway, I saw that a burning pine tree had fallen across it, preventing us from getting to the street. At first I thought, I have to drive over that, but I felt such intense fear—and shame about my fear—that I attempted a three-point turnaround so we could turn back, out of the fire.

I failed at turning around—my car got stuck. My back wheel was spinning, but we weren't moving. I could hear poor Izzy whimpering (the only other person in the car sharing my intense fear) but the other kids—Tommy, Violet, and Zara—were calm. I exclaimed "Okay, everybody out of the car—now!" I dropped my car keys to the ground outside my open door, but in that split second my only instinct was to grab the kids and run back up the driveway, perhaps to escape through the adjacent Frey Vineyards.

Izzy helped Violet and Tommy get out, and I ran around to Zara's car seat, fumbling with her buckles. Just as I pulled her out of her seat, I saw Jan's Subaru rushing toward us around the turn, and I instinctively yelled, "Help! Help!" even though I knew she couldn't hear me over the thunder of vacuumed air and flame-cracking trees.

But Jan stopped for us, and we all jumped in with Jan and her young dog Ruby. I immediately told Jan, "I love you!" and "I am so grateful for you!" and we sized up the burning tree in our path. She turned to me and asked, "Should we go for it?" As we got closer, we knew we couldn't make it over the tree. She jumped into reverse and raced backwards, somehow following the curves perfectly, passing my disabled car, driving in reverse for a quarter mile till we reached her driveway, where we could turn around.

We thought we could escape on the little dirt road that connects with Frey vineyards, but we realized that the fire had crossed Tomki there also, and our only recourse was to hurry back up the long driveway, three miles to our house, so I told Jan to let me drive. We switched positions, and I raced back up the road, so focused that I wouldn't allow myself to assess how close the fire was advancing; my goal was just to get back up the hill, but I recall three-year-old Zara saying in her normal, inquisitive voice, "Look, Mommy, that tree is on fire—and that one is on fire, and that one," over and over.

We saw my partner, Tom, in our old ranch truck, coming down the steep driveway. I tried to yell at him to go back up, but he didn't understand that a burning tree was blocking the road; he just thought a tree had fallen—a not-uncommon occurrence in late summer. He had a chainsaw and thought he could go clear the road, but when he went down a little farther, a wall of flames above Jan's place stopped him.

BILL TAYLOR: Original keyboard interlude: Mendocino Coast Storm excerpt.

MARY: shining water beads
across black charred trunk
strung on wispy web

On the long drive to Willits, I noticed the fire had moved down the ravines, creating triangles of brightness. I seemed to be in an altered state—calm, focused, but cotton-mouthed and so thirsty.

We had to stop to change a flat tire. By then we were almost in Willits, where we were able to get cell-phone reception. Ana's phone rang—it was Wes, my son in Potter Valley, who'd been worried that we hadn't evacuated, so he had tried to drive up Tomki to our house, only to discover that East and West Roads were both on fire, and county officials wouldn't let him up Tomki.

At that moment, he was driving out West Road, with flames on both sides. When I heard that, my already tumultuous stomach got worse—and the phone kept cutting out. Ana asked, "Are you safe? Are you safe?" When Wes finally answered, "Yes, I'm safe," I was flooded with relief.

JAELIN: hills scorched black and brown
patched with bright green
rain's first responders

I awoke smelling smoke at one a.m. on the morning of October 9, but I went back to sleep. Bill and I both woke up again at two a.m. to a black and red sky—FIRE! My body went numb in a way I never thought would be possible. What do we do? What do we need? I walked around for what seemed like hours but really was only minutes, picking up important papers and what little cash I had and placing it into an escape bag. I filled another bag with underwear, socks, changes of clothes, toothbrushes, and toiletries, and put them together. Then I got water and food.

Then something in my mind snapped, and I jumped into action—we have to save our place! "Bill, are you getting the firehose?"

"Yes."

"Call me when it's ready, and I'll turn it on."

Minutes later, I was outside by the spigot. Bill called, "Okay, turn it on!"

I did—and to my horror, water sprayed up like the Bellagio fountain, lit up by glowering red skies, but accomplishing nothing—the hose was full of holes! "This isn't working!" I shouted to Bill. "We need the garden hoses—all of them."

We decided which areas each of us would protect, and Bill patiently explained how to turn on the hose near the cabin where I stationed myself. But I couldn't understand him—it was as if he were speaking a foreign language. I screamed,

"I don't understand, Bill, show me how to do it!" He ran with me to the spigot and showed me. I grabbed the hoses, and Bill ran back to his hoses by the house.

We watered down the porches, the roofs, and the land surrounding them. I watered the road, where flying red embers blew in the terrifying wind. I'm here now, I thought. This is what I'm doing.... I'm insane to be here. Water everything. The dog is in the house, safe.... Wet the ground again; wet the sides of the cabin. Wet everything. Use whatever water is necessary. This is why we have water!

I shouted to Bill: "My hose won't reach! There's a fire on the ground!"

"Get it!" Bill called. He was on the phone with KZYX, and calling everyone we knew nearby to check on their safety.

"The hose won't reach—get here now! Please! I can't reach it!" The heat is intense. The wind is wicked. The mad fire crackles, wants so badly to burn everything. "Bill" I yelled again.

"I'm coming!" he yelled back.

His hose just barely made the distance, and he put the groundfire out. We then both went back to our posts—for however long I couldn't tell you; a couple of hours, many hours—with Bill calling out intermittently, "Be mindful of the water usage; I think we're out of danger now."

"I don't believe you, Bill! You said before that we were safe."

I kept on watering, soaking everything.

CHARLOTTE: black shadows in dirt
tracks coursing thru barren woods
melted water line

Back at our house, I ordered everyone to run in and put on hiking shoes and fill water bottles; I expected we would have to hike out the top of the property to a road accessible to Willits. I had an idea we could hike out via Siggy's house—our nearest neighbor above, who reaches her house from Willits.

Jan was still in her nightdress, but had some clothes in her car, so she got dressed while I ran upstairs to make some frantic calls. I called the Mendocino County Sheriff's Department to say that we couldn't get out. I wanted them to know we were stuck up the mountain. I also called neighbors to see if there was some escape route going uphill, even if we had to drive through a fence.

Then I ran down to let everyone know we should get going. By then Tom had returned in a state of complete shock, because he'd had no idea that the fire was on our property and that the road was hopelessly blocked. I told Tom we'd have to drive partway and then hike to Siggy's road.

The kids, Jan, Ruby, and I jumped into my old 4Runner. Tom gathered chainsaw and fuel; I grabbed some wet towels to breathe through, tossed them in a bag, and made sure the kids had good shoes and sweaters. Then we took off up the hill. Tom had to drive his old truck ahead of us way more slowly than I liked, and I was cursing at that truck to go faster!

We finally got to Rattlesnake Rock, the farthest we could drive toward Siggy's. We got out and Tom led the way as we bushwhacked on foot, down, through, and back up a heavily wooded canyon with sharp manzanita bushes and only faint deer trails that seemed to dead-end everywhere. Izzy bravely held Zara on her shoulders at times while also carrying her own backpack and ukuleles. Tom somehow brought us exactly to Siggy's property line, and then her back door—which was wide open, as if she'd left in quite a hurry.

We all caught our breath on Siggy's porch while Tom looked around for any extra cars and keys. Tommy was feeling anxious at this point, and needed a pep talk, so we calmed him down and talked about how, even if we had a long walk to Willits ahead of us, we knew we'd be okay. Poor Violet was crying about dropping her favorite doll along the way—the one she had knitted in handwork class at River Oak Charter School.

Jan, Ruby, the kids, and I got a head start on foot. In one of Siggy's sheds, Tom had found an all-terrain vehicle with keys in the ignition, and attached a small firewood trailer to it. He caught up with us and we piled in. Not much later, though, the trailer got a flat tire, and we realized that we weren't going much faster than walking speed anyway. Just then, we saw some figures ahead, watching us approach. I yelled in excitement that we had must have reached a neighbor of Siggy's who hadn't yet evacuated and might be able to drive us out.

The two men and young boy seemed strangely relaxed and calm, and puzzled by how eager we were to get moving. We tried to explain what was happening, and asked if they could please give us a ride to Willits. Finally, one of the young men offered to drive us. I begged Tom to come with us, but he refused. I knew he wouldn't go, so I didn't waste much time trying to persuade him.

The younger kids and Jan squished into the cab of the truck, and Izzy, Ruby, and I piled into the back. We raced to Willits, and though I knew we were on our way to safety, I was nervous about how fast we were driving over bumpy roads, and feared we'd be thrown from the truck. Izzy and I were cold in the open truck bed, and we huddled against the warm dog.

We finally got to a checkpoint, where sheriff's deputies told our driver where to take us. I tried calling Kim—Izzy and Tommy's mom—in Ukiah, thinking she'd be worried about us, but there was no phone service. I repeatedly apologized to Izzy. I felt ashamed, as if somehow it was my fault that we had encountered this life-threatening situation.

We finally made it to Willits. We were safe.

ROSS: plastic shrouds
covering car skeletons
by the roadside

In Willits, we went to the fire station to ask whether Highway 101 was open. Told that it was, we headed up to the top of the Willits Grade where, looking south toward Ukiah, we saw a lot of smoke. The road was open, though, and I thought that must mean it was safe to proceed, so we headed down the grade.

By the time we got to the section where there's only one lane and no way to turn around, the fire had crossed the freeway and was burning fiercely on both sides. The guardrail posts were aflame—but at that point, there was no turning back. In five minutes or so, we were beyond the inferno.

CATHY: The whole caravan made it to Willits, and some even made it down 101 to Ukiah before the highway was closed. I was relieved to reach a gas station, as my tank was near empty—I hadn't refueled after my drive to Santa Rosa. I remembered listening to a fire chief at a school assembly awhile back, lecturing about always keeping at least half a tank of gas in the car in case of emergency—and thinking at the time that he was just being alarmist.

By three or four a.m., Willits had opened its city hall as an evacuation center. Some of us checked in there, and were relieved to mentally check off friends and neighbors as they arrived. A large TV was broadcasting news of simultaneous catastrophic fires in Napa and Sonoma counties, but it gave us none of the news we yearned for—of what was happening in Mendocino County. It was crazy—fires jumping freeways, destroying shopping areas and neighborhoods, all happening at once. Were these fires stoppable? How long and how far till they were controlled?

Since 101 South was closed indefinitely by then, I decided—along with many other evacuees—to head to the coast from Willits and circle back to Ukiah. My dog, Terra, and I brought my neighbor, Jan, and her dog, Ruby, with us, and I heard more of Jan and Charlotte's harrowing escape. In Fort Bragg I got word that the horses had been found and were safe at the Ukiah fairgrounds.

I heard later that, around 10:30 a.m., while I was starting my roundabout route to Ukiah, Sarah was leaving there and heading back to Redwood Valley in another attempt to rescue the horses from the fire zone. She said, "We saw power lines and utility poles down; it was terrifying to drive over power lines that were still on fire. All along the way, we saw smoldering houses, completely flattened. Some spots were still actively on fire."

Sarah told me that they walked in through a still-hot, burnt-over vineyard to reach a creek bed below the barn area. There they found both her horse and mine, safe and uninjured, in a little patch of grass, everything around them completely burned.

CHARLOTTE: We arrived at the makeshift shelter at the Willits City Council chambers. Jan offered our driver some cash, and we ran in to see many familiar faces of our neighbors, plus several Buddhist monks and nuns from the monastery up the road. It was roughly three a.m. at this point, and we all huddled together, hoping the TV would tell us what was going on. Instead, we saw news reports of simultaneous shocking fires in Sonoma County—but nothing about Mendocino.

We had no cell-phone service, but one woman had a phone that got intermittent service, so we all took turns using it. I was finally able to get in touch with Kim, my stepchildren's mother, to let her know we were okay. She was very grateful. Everyone asked about Tom, and were shocked that he'd stayed behind. They looked at me with sorrow, thinking, I'm sure, that he wouldn't make it out of the fire alive. I remember Mimi's sweet daughter, Maria, stroking my hair and telling me it would be okay.

By daybreak, all the adults paced around each other like zombies. We were tired but still full of adrenaline, and wishing we could communicate with our families or find out what was happening with the fire. I had no idea whether or not Tom was okay, and no one had room in their vehicle for me and all four kids. Then our neighbors, Tombo and Willem, showed up and offered to squeeze us into their king-cab truck to go to the coast. We squished in and made the drive. It was lovely to be together and share our stories, and I looked forward to reuniting my stepchildren with their poor worried mother and older sister Graci.

We were a large caravan of evacuees. We made our first stop at Harvest Market in Fort Bragg, where we all regained cell service. Hundreds of messages piled in. I first called Tom, who said the fire was just below our house and coming up the canyon, and that he was ready with hoses. I begged him to leave, but he said at this point there was no way he could, since the fire had blocked the driveway. Shortly after that, we were on the road to Ukiah. While I was trying to occupy my children, I was also worried—I couldn't get any further response from Tom.

Kim came to retrieve her children, Izzy and Tommy, and let me know that Graci had just spoken with Tom. He said he was surrounded by fire and would be jumping into the pond. Again I feared that Tom really might not make it out. Kim and I cried and hugged, and then she left with the older kids. I then called the sheriff's department to let them know I was worried about Tom being surrounded with no way out, but just as I had almost finished giving them his information and location, he called me on the other line, so I told the sheriff's office to cancel the call.

Tom had made it through the initial firestorm that came up from the valley and canyon and around and through our homestead. He said he was okay, and that the main house was still standing, though one corner was smoldering.

The fire was now moving over the ridge behind and west of our place. The house was damaged but still standing. Tom described tons of "mini-campfires" burning all around and underneath the house, but he believed it would be okay. He couldn't talk long, as he had to get back to fighting the small fires that remained. Tom worked tirelessly, fighting hundreds of little fires for another twenty-four hours, till the pipes fully melted and disabled the hoses.

CLINT: I stopped when I reached Willits, and saw some of my neighbors pulled off the road together near the city park. We double-checked that everyone from the ranch was accounted for, then exchanged cell-phone numbers and tried to make a rough plan of how and where we could meet up.

As I got back to my vehicle, my friend, who worked for the Humane Society in Redwood Valley, said she thought she should get to the shelter and prepare to evacuate the animals. I said, "Well, then, let's go!" We pulled onto Highway 101 going south, and were soon headed down the Willits grade. We were the only vehicle on the road at 2:30 a.m., and at first I couldn't see much beyond my headlights.

As we descended it started to get smoky, then very smoky, and all of a sudden we were driving into the fire about halfway down the grade. Both sides of the road and the guardrails were on fire, and looking to the east I could see the mountain burning.

I continued south till I saw the edge of the fire, and suddenly we were through. I could see across the divide where the Highway Patrol and sheriff's officers were stopping northbound traffic. They were also trying to get a fuel truck to back down to a place where it could turn around.

Several miles later, we pulled into the animal shelter grounds. We went to the office to call other people to come help move about eighty cats and twenty-five dogs. I started putting together wire crates to load animals into, while staff and volunteers loaded up animals. It became apparent that the cats in their smaller crates could go in cars, but the dogs would need something bigger to accommodate them all.

My fourteen-foot trailer was parked at my shop, six miles away in Ukiah. I made a high-speed run, returned with it, and loaded all the dogs that had been crated. The last one was aggressive and wouldn't let anyone near it. It was a medium-sized animal, eyes wide in panic and lips curled back in a snarl.

I said calmly, "Please don't bite me; I just want to help you." I don't think it understood, but I was able to get the catchpole around its neck and lead it into its crate. Last dog on board! I drove to the Animal Control yard in Ukiah, where many people unloaded the animals to a temporary shelter that had been arranged. It was five a.m. I was tired but fully awake. I drove to my friend's house, and managed to get a couple of hours of sleep.

I awoke around eight a.m. and drove back north to Redwood Valley, but the roads had already been closed, so I couldn't go see if anything remained of the ranch—or if my two cats had survived.

NORI: At 1:30 a.m. I arrived at Jini and Peter's place at the top of Road B. Usually, as I drove up Road B, I would recall times past—all the various places I'd lived here along Salt Hollow Creek. On this late night, though, I did none of that. As I passed the oak tree in the middle of the road, across from the home where my son, Alder, was born, I didn't think about my time there living in a commune, milking goats, and raising my kids. My focus was elsewhere.

Like a robot I progressed up the hill, parked among the many other vehicles, and entered the home, where local neighbors and friends sat in shock and confusion about what was going on. On the TV were reports of fires in Santa Rosa and other places in Sonoma and Napa counties, but nothing here. Alder phoned to inform me that the Frey and Mariposa Ranches had also been evacuated. My heart sank. On the radio there was nothing but music. What is happening? Will the fires keep going? Is the world coming to an end?

We sat dumbfounded till it was determined that Jini and Peter also needed to evacuate. There were animals that need to be relocated, as well as the rest of us. I left for Alder's home, where his friends, other evacuees from Potter Valley, had arrived. No one was sleeping. Everyone was up, wondering what was next. My grandchildren, Finnley and Cassidy, were quite upset. They had been out on Tomki the previous day, visiting friends, and had left their bikes behind.

As daylight arrived, Alder and I went for a drive to see how far the fire had progressed. The next day, I learned that my place was gone. Over the next few weeks, I stayed at different places—friends were so welcoming and supportive. In mid-November, I landed for the next five months in a trailer at Jini and Peter's home, again at the top of Road B. Time to take a breath!

MARY: floating and drifting
misty clouds veiling hillsides
masking fire scars

Stupidly, I thought we'd be able to sleep that night, so I guided us to an inn in Willits. The night clerk, a young man from Redwood Valley, checked us in while he talked on the phone to the owner, who told him to raise the prices. As evacuees trickled into the lobby, though, the clerk continued to charge the normal rate. The next day, a new clerk took over and the prices went up—the young night clerk had been fired because he was, in his boss's words, "not a team player."

In the room, we were way too full of adrenaline to get any sleep. Hoping to get some news about Redwood Valley, we turned on the TV, but all they were showing was the Santa Rosa and Napa fires. Everyone began to call the Redwood Complex Fire "The Forgotten Fire" because for days the news focused only on the fires in Napa and Sonoma.

At the inn—and throughout Willits—phone lines were down, the Internet was down, and the gas supply in Willits was down. The hot water ceased. We ran into friends and neighbors eating breakfast or talking in the parking lot or on the balcony above us.

I felt a rush of gratitude and attachment for each person. It's a feeling I still have whenever I run into them, a feeling of appreciation for our shared experience that sometimes makes me teary just to think about.

ROSS: We got into Ukiah at three a.m. or so—but where to go? We called Orion, Ari's dad. No answer. We thought about going to a motel, but who could think of sleep? Somehow, the thought of pancakes and coffee seemed to hold the answer, so we pulled into Denny's, enticing Ari with the promise of hot chocolate. The couple in the next booth were talking about the sound of exploding propane tanks. We realized we weren't alone.

At 3:30 a.m. my cell phone rang. It was Susan Era, calling because the Pallesen family from the Fisher Lake subdivision across Tomki Road had arrived at her door, and Susan had immediately thought of us. "Yes, we're okay," I told her, "and consuming pancakes at Denny's—naturally!" Susan called Dan and Alese Jenkins, and they called and invited us to their place.

We did that, and fell into bed in their guestroom around five, wondering about our neighbors and our house, but quite happy to be alive and with friends.

CLINT: homes lost in wildfire
neighbor's rubble anchoring
season's first rainbow

MARY BUCKLEY: Original song (guitar and vocal): Scorched Earth

Reach your hand across the scorched-earth landscape of my life.
You may not ever understand, but I can see you care.
The deep and wondrous healing of the soul has just begun.
Thank you for being there.

Families went to bed that night on a hot and windy Sunday,
bellies full of home-cooked meals, heads full of plans for Monday.
The wind blew hard at midnight dark and broke an ancient oak
that fell on power lines that sparked and the valley filled with smoke.
The wind whipped up a firestorm taller than tall trees—
a howling inferno wherever it would blow—and it blew wherever it pleased.

Reach your hand across the scorched-earth landscape of my life.
You may not ever understand, but I can see you care.
The deep and wondrous healing of the soul has just begun.
Thank you for being there.

Shouts and horns and cell-phone calls, and letting the horses go;
grabbing children, shoes and keys—some stayed with just a hose.
Chaos and worry, confusion and hurry and car keys dropped in the dark;
embers whirling, thick smoke swirling—terror leaves its mark.

Reach your hand across the scorched-earth landscape of my life.
You may not ever understand, but I can see you care.
The deep and wondrous healing of the soul has just begun.
Thank you for being there.

Nature rages through the ages—treasures lost and great things gone.
Neighbor helping neighbor helping neighbor helping
neighbor is how we carry on.

Reach your hand across the scorched-earth landscape of my life.
You may not ever understand, but I can see you care.
The deep and wondrous healing of the soul has just begun.
Thank you for being there.
Thank you for being there.
Thank you for being there.

Intermission

BILL TAYLOR: Original instrumental keyboard music during intermission:
Midnight Malarkey

ACT II

KIM MONROE: I Don't Want Anything to Change by Bonnie Raitt

MARY: casting their needles
dying firs recovering
naked earth

Two days after the fire, we were able to drive down to Ukiah where we moved into friends' homes, first staying with Antonio and Muhasibi, and then renting from Marsha and Elliot. Other Redwood Valley friends were having trouble finding a place to move into, mainly because they had a German Shepherd puppy.

No one was allowed back into the burned area till ten days later. I was going to drive out there by myself one day, but I still felt quite vulnerable, and almost chickened out till an acquaintance said, "I'll go with you!" She kept insisting, so out Tomki we went. She was very excited, perhaps shocked, by the remains we saw along Tomki—a stone chimney, a garden table, miscellaneous things still standing. If I'd been moody or contemplative, there was no opportunity to feel it at that time. Later, I decided to go out there by myself, to just quietly look at what had been our life; to let some sadness sink in. It felt as if the trees had taken a last big breath and sucked up all the oxygen in their effort to survive. Every time Kim and I went back to our property, we felt breathless. All these months later, I still feel breathless just remembering it.

Book energy had abounded in our home. The books—no longer books but pages of ash, still holding their paper shape—lined up where the bookshelves used to be.

Someone asked if the trees were still standing. Of course plenty of black-trunked trees still stood, their dead branches drooping. The firs will most likely all die; hence we're doing salvage logging. It looks really barren where the fir forest was. The burned madrones and oaks and redwoods are sprouting, giving us hope for the recovery of the land.

Meanwhile, we'll try to restrain the brush that will want to take over, try to keep the poison oak and the star thistle down, and later replant oak trees.

ROSS: We crossed the creek nine times that night
while flames consumed our home.
I could have saved my laptop
But my mind was in a zone.
Escape is all that matters—Ari's life depends on us.
I miss my place like crazy, still,
But living's quite enough.

NORI: pulled from ashes
once useful things set aside
may be garden art

I found out on Tuesday that my place had burned down, but I couldn't return to the site till the following Sunday. I went there with my son, Alder, all suited up with boots, gloves, mask, rake, and shovel. Charlotte, my landlady before the fire, also returned with us. As I drove down the driveway, I could see that most of the trees had been felled. This was very sad, as they were large majestic oaks that provided much-needed shade. On the lower part of the property, where two oaks had been cut down, a Quan Yin statue stood on a stump, placed there by whoever felled that tree. Now with an open view, looking west into the valley, with a burned-out stove as a backdrop, I saw a photo opportunity. I began to take photos of the whole area, with one in particular of Charlotte from behind, seated in a chair as she gazed out at the charred landscape that had once been her home.

I began my archeological dig for treasures. Twenty minutes later, I was exhausted and felt sick to my stomach. I realized, after having found some jewelry, broken dishes, and a couple of things intact, that this process would be difficult and draining beyond belief. I came back five times that week and retrieved more pottery, jewelry, statues, and pieces of metal and glass—twisted and molded together by the heat. I decided to take these objects and make something from them. On Facebook I posted my desire to lead a mosaic workshop for those impacted by the fire, to take their found objects from the fire zone and recreate them into art pieces.

Metal and jewelry-making tools found in the remains of the home of Charlotte Healy, Nori's landlord. Photo by Ree Slocum.

I was surprised to find it was so difficult to decide what to make from my own retrieved items. My charred treasures sat, patiently waiting to be designed into something creative to place outside my new home. The workshop that Elizabeth Raybee and I led was fantastic; those who came to it made unique progress in their healing—and so did I.

CHARLOTTE: burnt-out stumps and roots
deep pits and traps underfoot
trees set to topple

The kids and I stayed at my parents' house in Ukiah for two or three weeks. I took only four days off work, and returned to complete a court trial exactly seven days after the fire. A group of women lawyers in the community gathered some work clothes for me, since mine were burned in my disabled car. It felt surreal to go back to work, walk into the courthouse, and be embraced by bailiffs, attorneys, court clerks, and at least one judge. I felt uncomfortable with the attention, but so grateful for the support.

My first trip back to see the property was eleven days after the fire. I went alone because I didn't want the kids to witness my emotional reaction. I was glad I did. The entire area was unrecognizable—I almost drove past my own driveway. The stench of burnt wood and plastic and particulate was terrible. Everything was charred black and gray. As I drove up the driveway, I saw the steel shell of my old

Two of the vehicles found destroyed near Jan Hoyman's home.
Photo by Ree Slocum.

vehicle, still sitting where we'd gotten stuck days earlier. Our house survived, only partly scorched, but the car with all the valuables I had tried to save was completely gone.

Driving farther, I could see that Jan's house had been destroyed, and it broke my heart. Inching my way up the road, I gasped at each turn. I was surrounded by hundreds of empty black holes, with smoke smoldering from burning stumps and roots below, and tall, blackened pine trees devoid of leaves.

By the time I made it to the house, though it was still standing, I was shocked to see a local forester and her work colleague inspecting our property for a salvage-logging operation. As they began to discuss those logistics with Tom, I burst into tears, feeling frustrated that I had to encounter this "business" discussion on my first trip up to my family home when I hadn't even had the opportunity to absorb my devastated surroundings.

During that first visit, I gathered some belongings and told Tom that it might be awhile before the kids and I could move back in. For a few days, I thought we might never want to move back there.

CATHY: yowling and yowling
cat tells fire stories when
evacuees return

The community animal rescue was immediate and awesome. My sheep had somehow dodged the flames, and happily wandered about my place, scavenging on downed trees and delivered hay. After a month or so, my cat timidly reappeared. Having lost two dogs and a cat to a house fire ten years prior, I was grateful that all my animals survived this time.

It was a couple of weeks before I was able to return to assess damages. As I'd been warned, all the structures had been destroyed except for two tindery sheds in the barn area that we would put to use for hay storage and sheep shelter. Most of my beloved woods was blackened—some areas bare to dirt. Trees with hollows had become chimneys, still smoking; others crisped to their tops—yet some areas were barely burned.

hungry survivors
sheep hay stacked by burned barnful
mice soon tunnel in

Changes soon started when rain arrived. Within a month there were signs of sprouting on the crisped redwoods. A strange bright-red fungus appeared in the hottest zones, along with thick green carpets of a moss known as bonfire moss. I had never dreamed that I would log my place, but salvage logging made sense with so many dead firs and pines. The big machinery of logging, PG&E, and FEMA cleanup crews became commonplace.

I stayed with my niece, Rose, in town, and then my sister, Marti, in Redwood Valley, but came back to the ranch daily to check on and feed my sheep. The FEMA crews especially enjoyed the sheep running up to greet my pickup with the hay delivery each morning, as I shouted, "Hey, sheep! Hey, sheep!" A PG&E tree worker rescued one sheep that tried to graze in the fishpond.

Photo by Ree Slocum.

With regular visits, I saw more signs of life returning daily: the brilliant green grass in the fields, and the soaproot leaves that helped feed my sheep; and from late January through May, a progression of wonderful wildflowers. Also making their late-January appearance, the first butterflies, especially the mourning cloaks, which winter over as adults and had somehow found protection from the fire. This resiliency of nature renewed me, along with the landscape.

A big emotional setback came, though, when I lost over half of my brave, fire-dodging sheep.

mourning cloak flutters
hovering above the sheep
mauled in dog attack

It started with two sheep missing; then, after fencing them for predator protection, I found them mauled by a dog attack. The routine changed to locking them inside the reinforced shed each night. I was so grateful that my brother, Tim, and a friend, Keith Leland, were willing to dedicate their time and skills to create a secure shelter while we waited for the vet.

There's so much to be grateful for, but I'm especially grateful for my temporary homes with my niece, Rose, and her partner, Chris, and with Marti and Jerry, who've accommodated me and my dog so graciously.

JAELIN: Three tomatoes hanging on a dried-up, scorched plant.
No green leaves, no succulent stems.
The ground was charred, with patches of dirt exposed.
But in this one little patch, between two formerly robust trees
with ripening fruit
A little tomato plant with just enough life in its veins
Summoned the energy to ripen these three small tomatoes.

CLINT: solid silver stream
from motorcycle meltdown
bright wildfire remains

I awoke around 8:00 on Monday morning and drove to Redwood Valley, but the roads had been closed, so I couldn't go see if anything remained of the ranch or if my two cats survived.

Two days went by, and I still couldn't go into the burnt area, but on the third day I was able to get past the road closures and see the ranch. The destruction was total, except for a couple of outbuildings that the fire chose not to take. Fires still smoldered against fallen trees, hollowed-out root crowns, and the piles of coal that used to be our homes. Strange things still sat, basically unburnt, with burned land completely surrounding them: a pickup truck, a bench in a field, a chainsaw on a wooden sawhorse right next to what used to be a cord of oak firewood, now com-

Photo by Ree Slocum.

pletely evaporated to ash. Every random thing I found became a small victory, and a wonderment at the power of fire.

As I walked through the ashes of the ranch, I became filled with certainty that this was not the end of this ranch or community—that although it seemed bleak and terrible, something amazing was going to come from this. I would make sure of it! I owed at least that much to this place and these people.

MARY: The adrenaline kept me rolling for quite a while, till all of a sudden my energy just gave way. I had a dream that I was climbing a ladder and it kept sinking into the ground.

We moved into the Sky House thirty-eight years ago, when Ben was just six months old. How does one rebuild a home when one is sixty-eight and the children are no longer little 'uns in the home who create laughter and yell and stomp and fight and make sword-swishing noises and engine noises, and fall asleep while I read to them, or make animal pancakes on a Sunday morning? What sparkles of energy filled that house, after baby showers and disastrous slumber parties and holiday meals with everyone crowded into our little kitchen!

What I miss the most after the fire is my sense of home and community. Our friends and neighbors are flung to the four directions.

Now I flit around town, seemingly impervious to all the stress, but it's there, and it catches me in quiet moments. You'd think that after all this time life would be easier. I look like I'm fine, but it's up and down. Simple life stresses hit me like they never used to.

Sometimes my word of the day is "disoriented," some days it's "numb," some days "sociable," and sometimes it might be "verging;" verging on what, I cannot say—tears, hope, normalcy, some kind of certainty. This morning it was definitely "quandaries," so many quandaries, buried in quandaries, heavy with quandaries. Dealing with insurance—will we rebuild, how will we rebuild, what about the septic tanks, the water? Who am I? Where am I going to land?

Then, with the help of some coffee and a morning bun at Black Oak and a short visit with Clint, I snap out of it; then Estelle shows up and makes me feel lighter. Thanks, Clint and Estelle!

CLINT: Instrumental jazz guitar: Amazing Grace

CATHY: The impact of this fire for me and my neighbors is huge and long-lasting. So many stories of narrow escapes and, sadly, of lives lost. The first few months after the fire found me euphoric that so many of us survived—yet I also felt a bit adrift. Then, so many choices to make, navigate a new life, restore a blasted landscape!

I am so appreciative of the safety net cast by a caring community. Through this support, I've found resources and opportunities to move forward. Though challenging circumstances require many revisions in my life, I still count my blessings.

CHARLOTTE: The kids and I moved back three weeks after the fire, just before my forty-second birthday, Halloween eve. We were really excited and ready to go home. The kids seemed content, immediately accepting the changed landscape. I think all that mattered to them was having their same toys and familiar home surroundings, and for this I'm so grateful. Of everyone in our family, I'm the one who's struggled most with all the changes.

For the next nine months, my little family, while incredibly grateful to still have our home, had to learn to navigate the cleanup process, dealing with various layers of government coordination. We had to share the roads with unfamiliar people and vehicles daily. At one point, at the end of the FEMA/Army Corps cleanup, Zara, then three years old, was so used to me referring to the dump trucks as "FEMA" that she said to me, "Mommy, where is FEMA? Did she go home?"

From late December till early February, we had to use snow chains on our trucks to make it home, because of the runoff of silty erosion. The dirt road became a glue-like mess of mud that even my new four-wheel-drive truck couldn't escape. On more than one occasion, I got stuck with kids in the car. I would have a panic attack each time, as I relived the fear of being stuck in my car with the kids, surrounded by fire. My heart would race, and my eyes would fill with tears in relived panic, as well as frustration with the new status quo.

We also had to coexist with a massive salvage-logging operation, which only stopped for the summer in June. Every day, I felt a rush of fear-filled adrenaline as I drove up and down my narrow dirt driveway, afraid I'd encounter a large strange vehicle. Don't get me wrong: the individual workers were nothing but kind; but it was still scary for me on that road with my car full of little children.

I started to leave my house by 6:45 a.m. each day to take the kids to school and go to work, in hopes that I could avoid being stuck on our property as heavy equipment and log trucks obstructed our way. As the days lengthened later in spring, however, the log trucks barreled up the mountain earlier and earlier, and I'd pray they would wait for us to get by.

At night, when we came home from work and school, we'd discover more huge changes in the landscape, more trees felled and gone, and even the road itself altered here and there.

NORI: Seven years old, I climb onto the hard leather slung seat at the long mahogany dining table my grandpop designed and built. My chin almost rests on the tabletop, and my legs dangle off the edge, as if I were teetering on a cliff face.

Grandpop described how he came up with the design of this table and the six matching chairs, a cross between Lodge and Mission styles, with a dash of contemporary art deco. I listen intently while I enjoy my barbecued chicken.

Flash forward fifty-eight years: It's a sweltering summer afternoon. Having just cooled off in the pool, I sit at the dining-room table and jot down a few creative ideas. I jump up as I realize my wet derriere has created a heart-shaped mark on the leather seat of Grandpop's chair. I'm upset with myself, as this will be a permanent mark.

Flash forward six weeks: I lay the completed application for the Golden Rule Mobile Village on Grandpop's mahogany table, and go to bed listening to the wind howl. I'm fearful a tree might fall on my place; I've never experienced gusts like this here before.

Flash forward six more months: I sit on a leather chair—part of the set of six that Grandpop made to go with his mahogany table. This particular chair had been in storage; it has a large mark on it, from someone having sat on it in wet clothing, but because it was in storage, it didn't burn like the other chairs did, along with the mahogany table and everything else in my place.

I feel comforted, sitting in this leather slung seat. I begin to explore more creative ideas as I sit here, just as my grandfather once did.

MARY: in the checkout line
another neighbor's stories of
fire and sleepless nights

Writing has been my therapy—much of it on Facebook. As I laughed and cried, my stomachaches went away. I noticed there were others who want to write about their fire experience, so I started a writing group. I thought we'd collect all sorts of fire stories; instead we write and rewrite our deepest thoughts and feelings, poetry, narratives, stream-of-consciousness. Dee Cope was inspired to write about the things we had, rather than to grieve their loss, to focus on enjoying what we remember. My home, the Sky House, was filled with stories—in things that belonged to my mother, or that Kim and I brought back from Africa—so many things that connect me with people and places. And now I attempt to write those stories.

Kim and I started saying to each other, "Isn't it great? We don't have to worry about that pile of papers on the massage table anymore."

"We don't have to go through those boxes of old supplements and medications."

"We don't have to worry about the deer in the garden. There is no garden!"

I asked others on Facebook to tell me their examples of things we no longer have to worry about. Clint said:

CLINT: Building a new deck on the east side of your house. On second thought, I'm still going to have to build that deck—I just have to build a house for it to hang off of first.

I've been building and working in construction my entire adult life, learning everything I needed to know about how to bring a place like this back from disaster. This is what I intend to do.

JAELIN: I will dearly miss my friend and former neighbor, Char Foster, who loved and supported everything Bill and I did, and moved away after losing her home. I so miss my cats, L.C. and Shorty, who died in the fire. I also miss the beautiful, stately, embracing oaks and pines and Douglas firs that lined our road and dotted our landscape and the paths along our property. I'll miss my neighbors, Laura and John's, lovely straw-bale house. I miss the hand-split rail fence that my neighbor, Robert, made himself; it surrounded his garden and the outside of his home, along a short stretch of common road. It was one of the selling points when we moved to this land. I will dearly miss my friend and neighbor, Vicki, stopping to chat when our cars met on the road, rather than just quickly passing each other. We'd catch up on the neighbors and family business and other things. I miss being eager to work and paint, and having the landscape call, "Paint me! Paint me! For God's sake, paint ME!" I miss my neighbor, Chuck's, twin palms. I miss the brush and man-zanita forest on our ridge, the one where the bears loved to forage for berries.

I miss my feeling of security, of at long last finding a place where I

Photos by Cathy Monroe.

can feel safe and protected. I miss my sense of well-being, and maybe my arrogance in thinking that we live in the greatest place. I miss the thought—now fantasy—that my sister, Silvia, will come out to California and live with us. Since the fires, she has no interest in doing that at all.

What I don't miss are the huge numbers of ticks that may have died in the fire. Unless I'm imagining it, it seems as if their population is lower this year.

CATHY: I miss my woods, with trees draped or splattered with lichens and moss. I especially miss some of my large, imposing oaks and madrones, with their pools of shade. Of course, I miss my new home, which Clint built to replace the one that burned in 2007. It was a unique custom yurt that fit me perfectly. I miss my twice-daily visits to the huge redwood barn that had loomed up like a ship for a century, with its countless woodpecker holes. When I went to feed at night, the barn's lights would shine out through the holes, looking like stars shining out from inside the barn to join the stars in the heavens.

What I won't miss: I won't miss my accumulation of things that "might" still be useful—boxes of stuff like clean jars, and yogurt and cottage-cheese containers, or "only slightly leaky" raingear. I won't miss the guilt of not keeping my fine saddles and tack in good working order. I won't miss the paintings that I couldn't quite get right, hoping to work them over someday. I won't miss the invasion of poison oak and blackberries in my garden—because, undaunted, they're still there.

And speaking for my dog, she has mostly enjoyed the change in her situation. She's included in most of my activities now: she goes to meetings and yoga class, enjoys leashed walks in town that offer a richness of sniffs and endless canine messages, and of course our regular inspections of ranch activity. She doesn't miss the life of a stay-at-home dog.

ROSS: I miss my musical instruments, especially my violin. It had a sound and feel that I loved. Also my Martin guitar, though I'm somewhat looking forward to getting a smaller one with easier action for fingering.

I think about all the family photographs that are gone; especially the ones from when Orion and David and Erik were kids. In a way those are the biggest loss, because they're irreplaceable. Another thing I miss is my wood-burning stove, and the feel of wood heat permeating our bedroom. As fate would have it, I had the nicest stack of firewood in many a year, all cut, split, and stacked, set for winter last year. We had a nice house where we stayed after the fire, but turning on a thermostat for forced-air heating just wasn't the same.

What I don't miss is mouse poop. We lived in a very old house that we loved in many ways, but one way I didn't love it was how well it offered little creatures an opportunity to enter and explore for food and shelter.

Through ardent effort, we had gotten it pretty mouse-proofed most of the time, but the work to keep it that way was a bit of a hassle. The experience of living there for eighteen years brought the realization that ultimately the mice would win! No matter how many nooks and crannies we stuffed with steel wool or expando-plastic goo, eventually there would be some entry point. Then the telltale droppings would appear to remind us that, as much as we love and appreciate the natural world in all its amazing diversity, we also appreciate certain boundaries.

CHARLOTTE: Things I do not miss: Tom's sheds full of disorganized tools. Recycled glass containers full of nails and screws. Odd-shaped, discarded windows and things Tom intended to repurpose. The old Chevy pickup truck that hasn't run in twenty-five years. Tom's motorcycles—of course he would beg to differ! Boxes of old paperwork I had intended to shred....

It was as though someone had vacuumed our entire homestead, making it possible to discover the amazing topography beneath years of wild brush; cleansing and making room for the most incredible cycle of spring wildflowers.

NORI: Things I will not miss: The large pinecones falling and barely missing my head. Pine sap dripping onto my car. Having a bathroom detached from my place.
I'm so thankful for my family's and my friends' financial and emotional support, and especially to my son, Alder, who has helped fix up my new home at Golden Rule Mobile Village.

I'm thankful for the Redwood Valley Grange and the California State Grange, which provided a place to go after the fire; and for food, massage, clothes, and general support.

I'm thankful to Jini and Peter Reynolds for their kindness, and for providing me a place to lay my head for months after the fire.

What can I say about our community? So many people stepping forward to listen, help, donate, and support all those who lost things in this fire. There is a silent sense of understanding among those of us who lost our homes, family members, animals—another connection that holds us together as we move forward!

MARY: It's the connection with people, and the beauty of earth and art that give me hope. The emotions triggered by people's thoughtfulness, generosity and compassion help release my trauma, make me cry or laugh and get it out!

Every time I use one of the scarves or earrings, clothing, placemats, ceramic bowls, and dishes that people have given to me, I think of them. Sometimes it also makes me grieve the loss of things I had before, particularly the handmade items.

Little by little, I'm collecting treasures—a Jan Hoyman cup gifted by Marilyn Zensen; bowls from Diane Clifton; plates from Ruth Easterbrook; a painting by Adele Pruitt of the oak tree at the ranch, where Ben and my nephew Ian had their weddings....

People! I've never felt so connected, in such a vulnerable, deep, and meaningful way. Thanks for the generosity of the greater Ukiah community; the many friends and acquaintances who welcomed people into their homes; family and friends from all over the globe who reached out with concern and support and love. Just reading this again, the tears well up.

Thanks to Sharon, who lifted the beautiful green silk scarf off her neck and draped it around me. Thanks to Chris and Cassie Gibson, who lent Kim a guitar and fed and clothed us. A special thank you to my yoga teachers, Maggie and Genevieve, who helped me breathe deeply again and showered me with gifts.

CHARLOTTE: fire-lost cherished puppets
returning as Christmas gifts
unexpected tears

We've desperately missed having neighbors. Even though we're so remote—"that weird, isolated family up the hill"—and had never felt fully accepted into the social fabric of our Tomki community, we still felt camaraderie when we'd encounter our neighbors in their vehicles on the driveway below or on the road. Now I feel a sense of closeness and acceptance in the social fabric, because the fires intertwined everyone so closely.

There's also a sense of hope, as we see houses slowly constructed along West and Tomki roads. More recently, a family whose rental burned at Mariposa Ranch has been at work on a water system. They plan to move back to a spot below Jan's place.

We're so excited to see them, and can't wait to have neighbors again. Perhaps what I've really missed is the sense of knowing there's someone I can call—or who can call me—if we encounter an emergency in the future. It's good to know we're not alone!

A lovely takeaway from the fire is the pride and love I feel for my neighbors and for the greater Mendocino County community: first, of course, for Jan, who arrived at just the moment when my family needed her; for the bravery of my children and their father, and our great teamwork; for my fellow Mendocino County employees, who were among the very first to arrive at the shelter after our escape, and treated us with such dignity and respect; for the tireless work of countless volunteers who are still helping everyone; for the contractors who helped clean up and are now rebuilding Redwood Valley; and for the extensive services provided to fire survivors by the county and nonprofit agencies.

We really are blessed to live in such a close community.

NORI: Draped in feathery pine, dappled by oak leaf, I sit; grass gently sways to a slight flow of late-spring air. I sit on a bench at Mariposa Ranch; it's weathered, yet strong. It still stands, not having been scorched by the dragon's fire that roared through here just months ago.

As I sit quietly next to the Diogenes' lanterns and an oak gall, I wonder, Who sat on this bench? I sit among the grasses and wonder, Who walked here many moons ago, when wildlife was plenty and acorns were flushed out in the creek? I sit among the singing winged creatures, and I wonder, Have their songs changed over time? Are there more alarm calls now than back then? As I sit here, I wonder, Who gave birth on this land? Who died here? Who sat here, draped, like me, in feathery pine, dappled by oak leaf?

JAELIN: up deeply burned trunks
tender green sprouts emerging
sempervirens

Everything works holistically, a little of this and a little (or a lot) of that. Healing is that way too. This past year, I've been fortunate to have my therapist, Margaret, very available; she is wise, kind, and very understanding. My recent good fortune also placed me in the capable hands of both Nori Dolan and Elizabeth Raybee. I took part in a three-day workshop on mosaics that they facilitated free for fire survivors, and held at Elizabeth's grand new studio in Ukiah.

Until a few months ago, I hadn't done anything besides being in therapy to help with the trauma of having gone through three fires last year. Then I registered for business coaching, and said, "I've lost my rudder. I used to be able to say I'll do something, and just get it done. That's not happening this year—I feel as if I'm swimming upstream in a bubble of Jell-O. Help!"

One project I was particularly committed to was the promotion of my first storybook. I would have liked to continue promoting it, but honestly, the fires took a lot out of me. I was left emotionally and physically spent, bereft of energy.

Because of some great, kind act of fate, I'm blessed with a loving, intelligent husband and a warm, open community to help me through what I'd otherwise consider a year in flames. I am so grateful for the kindness and generosity of our community. I will always remember them. They offered so much support of every kind.

ROSS: Many factors have contributed to the recovery process. The main one is the people of the community coming together in recognition of the loss and in offering support. The gratitude that comes from being a recipient of the support is something that, in a strange way, is like a benefit of the whole event.

Disaster can bring out the best in people, and I can't help but feel that I'm lucky to live in this community where so many people are motivated by a desire to help. Here are a few of my experiences of that.

Financially: Community organizations and businesses have stepped up with all kinds of assistance, from direct cash grants to clothes, furniture, counseling, and more. My wife, Charlotte, and I are especially grateful to North Coast Opportunities, Redwood Credit Union, Red Cross, The Rotary Club, Raley's, the Redwood Valley Grange, and the Community Foundation of Mendocino County.

Neighborhood get-togethers: All the houses in our old neighborhood were destroyed. Now, on an informal whoever-can-make-it basis, a bunch of us have been getting together once a week for pizza and a beer and/or just to chat.

Housing: We're in our fifth living situation since the fire. The first was staying with friends for a week. Then we were connected to folks who offered us their house for a couple of weeks while they were away. Then we were offered a room with friends, who'd also lost their homes, in a big house they were renting. We stayed there a month and then, through another friend, we were offered a house to housesit for five months. Now we're in a rental owned by Marsha and Elliot, very fire-survivor-sensitive folks who are renting it to us on very reasonable terms.

MARY: Things we do now—things that feel normal—help me feel better about whatever is to happen in the future. We had the Solstice Bonfire in December. We hosted a Christmas-morning brunch that we used to hold at Cathy's home.

I told my grandson shortly after the fire that we'd most likely get another four-wheeler, and last weekend we took both grandsons for a ride in our new one. We played in the creek, just like we used to. We swam in the pool—yes, that survived. We've been meeting our neighbors out there late in the day to cool off.

NORI: What's the most decadent thing you've done since the fire?

"Me?" you ask. Wine, cheese, olives, marinated artichokes... soaking in an outdoor jacuzzi and listening to the waves crash on a secluded Mendocino County beach. Oh, the healing! Oh, the respite! Oh, the melting into the cavern of creativity! Sun-seated, with a view of the sea and its calm waves as I ease into the evening. It's warm. I've bathed in the chorus of singing waves and winged conversation. Oh, to tap into the well of liquid luxury!

CLINT: I'm grateful to feel like I got to live through and be a small part of the history of the ranch and Redwood Valley as a whole. In the months after the fire, I've never felt more connected and grateful to my friends and neighbors. Though I'm sad for all our losses, I'm grateful to go through this together with everyone on the ranch. I feel bonded to them in a way that's hard to describe, except to say, "This is where I belong."

JAELIN: I saw a baby bear walking on our road! He or she scampered away before I could grab a photo. I really didn't care about that, though, it was just a wonder to behold. My heart felt warm and overjoyed to see that little bear, looking fat, with a thick, healthy, shiny coat of fur. Yay! Bears are here!

I love you, Baby Bear, and Mama Bear, and all of your bear family. I'm glad that you're able to find enough food here, and shelter too, amidst the burnt brush and altered forest and landscape. Earlier this morning, walking on our burnt land, I just wanted to run far, far away, until I saw you and wondered, Would my neighbors protect you if I left? I feel as if I have to take care of you—and maybe even stay here after all.

Stay here and grow fat and make babies, little bear. Keep your family going. I'll do my best to stay on the ranch, even though part of my heart still wants to go far, far away.

MARY: I've been watching the landscape change and recover. I've already learned to appreciate the altered view across the valley. What will happen to all those burned trees? Will they fall soon, or stand as reminders of our firestorm?

I've been spending some time mowing and weed-eating near the Enchanted Canyon, where Mariposa Creek runs. When I get worn out, I just sit on the ground and listen, and look around. I can still hear the sounds of water bubbling and birds singing. This last spring, there were so many wildflowers, and some of the trees are still green!

The new view. Photo by Ree Slocum.

What a Spring! Photo by Mary Monroe.

We don't have a home yet, but I do have hope.
CHARLOTTE: generosity
community heart to heart
resuscitation

CATHY: so painfully sweet
the deeply piercing contact
of our hearts touching

ROSS and MARY BUCKLEY: Lean on Me by Bill Withers

CAST (and audience) joins in on the chorus:
"Lean on me when you're not strong...."

—END—

List of Contributors